Successful Media Relations

Successful Media Relations

A practitioner's guide

Judith Ridgway

Gower

Published by
Gower Publishing Company Limited,
Gower House, Croft Road, Aldershot,
Hants GU11 3HR, England

Gower Publishing Company,
Old Post Road, Brookfield,
Vermont 05036, USA

Library of Congress Cataloging in Publication Data

Ridgway, Judith
　Successful media relations.

　Includes index.
　1. Mass media and business.　2. Public relations.
　I. Title.
　HD59.R48　1984　659.2　84-6128

British Library Cataloguing in Publication Data

Ridgway, Judith
　Successful media relations.
　1. Public relations
　I. Title
　659.2　HM263

ISBN 0 566 02469 1

Printed in Great Britain by Dotesios (Printers) Limited,
Bradford-on-Avon, Wiltshire.

Contents

Introduction

Successful media relations involves understanding the media, how they work and what their requirements are. It also involves relating this knowledge to the needs of your own organisation and the objectives of its media relations programme.

This book is essentially practical. It is concerned with the tools, the organisation and the planning of the media relations programme. But it also seeks to show how a thorough knowledge and understanding of the media can make your efforts much more effective.

There is, after all, no point in spending a fortune on trying to communicate an important story if you are telling the wrong people, in the wrong way, at the wrong time. Putting yourself in the recipient's place and deciding exactly what will be of interest and what will not, will be much more useful from everyone's point of view.

This kind of practical knowledge of the media will put you in a much better position to build up a harmonious and helpful relationship with those sections of the media which cover your organisation's particular activities. And this relationship will in turn help you to establish a smooth communications channel between media and management.

Unfortunately the senior managements of some organisations tend to view the press or media relations department as a buffer between the media and themselves. This can only lead to trouble. Very often the PRO is not qualified to answer detailed and possibly highly technical questions. Nor does he or she have the authority to answer for the company on important issues. Such an attitude inevitably leads to an unnecessarily bad press and a lack of co-operation by the media on future occasions.

Rather, the PRO should be the means by which the two sides can talk to each other more easily and with more understanding. You must stick to your professional guns in telling senior management what the consequences of their actions in the media relations field are likely to be. You must, however, also follow up such a stand with sensible advice on dealing with the media and be on hand to see fair play.

Of course there are occasions when certain sections of the media behave with some dishonesty and as PRO you must watch out for signs of such a situation arising and warn your management in time. But the vast majority of dealings with the media will not be like this, and management must be encouraged to be as open as possible.

Building up a favourable relationship with the media often involves building up a good personal relationship with key journalists in your field. You cannot hope to achieve this if you are not convinced yourself. If you do not think that you can be committed to an organisation's activities do not work for it. Honesty is as important at this level as it is on individual issues.

This applies equally whether you are planning to work directly for the organisation or for its PR consultants. Indeed everything in the book applies to both situations, for they differ only in their organisation and lines of control. To all intents and purposes a PR consultant must act as though he or she works directly for the client organisation. 'Public Relations Officer' has also been taken to be synonymous with 'Press Relations Officer' for the purposes of this book.

Of course a harmonious relationship with the media does not mean that everything will always go smoothly. Sometimes your objectives and those of your media friends will be in conflict and this is where your powers of diplomacy will be tested to the full. Competent journalists will be critically probing. That is *their* job. *Yours* is to present the facts in the most favourable light for your organisation and, if the problems are severe, to ensure that ultimately your organisation's worst story receives the best hearing.

A good example of successful media relations concerns a multinational oil company, one of whose oil tankers was wrecked, causing extensive spillage along the Californian holiday beaches. Sales at petrol stations immediately started to fall. The company instituted an expensive and wide-ranging mopping up programme including very quick cleaning of the popular beaches and a bird sanctuary, and a marine life survey and restocking operation.

Full details of the disaster and the company's very prompt action were relayed to the media at once and this, coupled with the previously good relationship between the oil company and the media, ensured that most of the coverage was concentrated on the mopping up operation. The result was that the company was seen as a responsible, socially conscious organisation rectifying an inevitable disaster, rather than as an irresponsible multinational with no concern for the environment. The sales not only recovered but exceeded the previous norm.

There are times when the disaster is less obvious to the public view and this is when there is a strong temptation to deny everything. The short answer is, don't – and don't allow your management to do so either. If you or any of the representatives of your organisation do lie, your reputation in the media will be shattered and its loss will precede you into whatever industry you go. It is very rare for the truth not to emerge, given time, and once a journalist has been castigated by his editor for believing your lies he will, understandably, never trust you again. He will be suspicious of everything you and your organisation have to say and will tell his associates to be wary too.

Successful media relations, then, means understanding the people with whom you want to communicate – producers, editors and journalists – appreciating their problems, needs and audiences and treating them with honesty, efficiency and common sense. It is this principle that underlies all the detailed information and advice to be found in the pages that follow.

1 The media relations programme

The term 'media relations' refers to the communication pattern between an organisation and those sections of the media which are interested in its activities. Such communication may be concerned with anything and everything which happens within and around that organisation. It may also be concerned with local and national issues, with finance and legislation and with public opinion.

Communication between organisation and media may be initiated by either side, but from the organisation's point of view media relations is concerned with achieving the most favourable coverage possible. This can sometimes be achieved by reacting to individual happenings or to media enquiries but at best this approach is haphazard and at worst it is inefficient and potentially dangerous.

It is far better to plan a media relations programme within the framework of your organisation's objectives as a whole. This not only helps to channel your efforts into the most effective areas, but also ensures that everyone who comes into contact with the media knows what their organisation is trying to achieve.

Making a plan

The first step is to define and analyse the problems and then to set objectives to be achieved. The problems will of course vary according to the field in which your company or organisation is operating and what it is trying to achieve. However, for a manufacturing company the problems might include any of the following:

- The product range is seen as too expensive.
- The proper use of a new product is not really understood.
- The company has a reputation for bad service.
- The company is moving into a new high technology field and needs to upgrade its scientific image.
- The company is not thought of as a good employer.
- The more expensive end of the product range is not being retailed through the right kind of outlets.
- There is a major technical development behind the introduction of a new product which is not fully appreciated.
- The company is thought of as being old fashioned.

All these and other problems will come in as feedback from the marketing and other departments. Obviously they need to be countered and an objective must be set. Ideally objectives should be measurable and they should be achievable. If you set unobtainable objectives you will be seen to have failed even if you do a wonderful job. To some extent this is also true if the objectives are not measurable.

Whatever you do, do not try to link your objectives to sales. There may be a great temptation to try and do this as part of a justification for the very existence of the media relations programme. But you are very unlikely to be able to show a link which is directly attributable to your activities and you will be encouraging the view that media relations is simply a cheap form of advertising.

If an objective is to be effectively measured it needs to be very clearly defined. There is no point in stating that the objective is 'to increase awareness' or 'to change an attitude'. This is not enough. You must include the answers to the questions 'of what?' and 'by whom?', which will lead you into defining your target audiences. The answer to 'who are you trying to influence?' will in turn lead you on to 'how are you going to reach them?', and once you have reached this stage the programme starts to become practical.

Analysis

Here's a very simple example of the start of a media relations programme for a small company producing torches.

The problems

Market research has shown that the company's torches are seen as dependable but rather old-fashioned and there is little awareness of the newer products which have been introduced to fit the contemporary lifestyle.

Objectives

1 To increase awareness of the more recent products.
2 To show that these products are up to date and invaluable to the modern man or woman.
3 To give the company a more go-ahead image, while retaining the dependable aspect.

Ultimate target audiences

The torch-buying public includes the following markets:
(a) Women buying torches for domestic and car use.

(b) Men buying torches for similar uses.
(c) Industrial buyers for watchmen and security services.
(d) The police and the armed services.

Intermediary target audiences

The media reaching the ultimate target audience include the following groups:

(a) Women's interest programmes and publications.
(b) Men's and general interest programmes and publications.
(c) Motoring programmes and press and the caravan and holiday press.
(d) Security and safety publications (both consumer and trade).
(e) Police and armed services press.

Action

This sort of analysis makes the rest of the programme much easier to plan. Working against the background of known developments and plans for the torch company for the coming year a single idea for each area will start the programme off. There may, for example, be plans to launch a new pocket or handbag version of one of the company's torches; if it is sufficiently different from anything else on the market this could form the basis for an onslaught on the women's interest press.

The frustration of life without a torch, illustrated by either a feature or a demonstration, could interest the men's press, and special car fitments for fixing a torch inside the car would be of great interest to the motoring media. Similar ideas for features, visits and events could be thought up for the remaining areas.

A plan like this not only shows up the priority areas and assists a sensible organisation of the workload; it also shows where effort should be concentrated and helps in the measurement of success.

Massive coverage may look good but it is a lot less valuable if it appears in media which are not seen by your ultimate target audience. There could even be occasions when extended coverage in a large number of regional and provincial newspapers is much more useful than a short piece in *The Times*. The temptation is, of course, to impress management with national press coverage, but this may not always be the most effective. It may be good for your ego, but is it good for the company?

Once you have an outline of your media relations programme worked out, and preferably written down, you will be ready to start thinking about the detailed use of tools such as media lists, press releases, competitions, press receptions, workshops, visits and special events. All of them are dealt with in detail in the chapters that follow.

Summary of Chapter 1

1   It is much more effective to carry out media relations activities within the framework of a detailed plan than simply to publicise events as they happen and haphazardly respond to media enquiries.
2   Start by defining and analysing problem areas and set communication objectives to be achieved.
3   Define the target audiences, both primary and intermediary, for your publicity message.
4   Plan activities which can be used to communicate that message to those targets.
5   Start to assess the relevance of the plans to the stated objectives. Will coverage be achieved in the most effective areas?

2 Lists and contacts

The media comprise literally thousands of publications and hundreds of TV and radio stations in the UK alone. Every time something newsworthy happens in your organisation you will need to consider which of these many outlets are likely to be interested in the information. In most cases the answer will include only a fraction of the total. It is therefore very useful to make up lists of those outlets which you may want to contact regularly. This saves the chore of going through large media directories every time you want to contact the media. Sometimes you may want to reach everyone on the list, but more often you will only be using certain sections or even picking out a dozen or so specialist outlets.

Compiling media lists

Uses for the media list

The first step in compiling a media list is to define the uses to which it will be put. Once this has been done it is relatively easy to list the relevant media for each type of activity. Such an exercise not only pinpoints the media which will be of interest to you but also helps in classifying the list in the most helpful way.

It is worth reiterating here the point that the media offer a means of influencing your target audiences. Depending on the particular objectives of the public relations programme, these audiences may include potential or existing customers, creditors and shareholders, schools or other educational bodies, employees, local residents, government and other authorities and opinion-formers in the appropriate fields.

In trying to reach any of these groups you will need to study the media in some detail. The audience and readership profiles of the various media will help to determine which of them should be included on your list and which can be safely left out.

The media cannot operate without input and you will need to provide them with something of interest to impart. This may not be hard news in the sense that it would be of interest to the news desk of the daily newspapers, but it must have something to interest a specific readership.

In fact almost everything that happens within your organisation could be of interest to the right publication. All of the following activities will give rise to a need to communicate with the media and therefore the need for a carefully selected list of those who will be interested. Add to or subtract from this list according to the needs and activities of your particular organisation.

- Launch of a new product or service
- Initiation of new factories or offices

- Financial results
- Sponsored events, awards and charitable activities
- Launch of promotional campaigns
- Disasters, strikes and closures
- Awards and accolades for the company or organisation
- Visits of dignitaries or celebrities, or press facility visits
- Important orders and exports
- Compilation of background feature material
- Scientific or technical advances
- Appointments at all levels
- Publication of survey or market research material
- Small changes in prices, products and services
- Involvement in local activities

Each of these activities offers a newsworthy vehicle for furthering your objectives vis-à-vis your various target audiences.

How to find the information

There are a number of reference works which can be used to study the media. They vary in the type and quantity of the information they give and you may need to use two or three different directories to make an accurate analysis of the media which will be valuable to your organisation.

Names and positions are as important as addresses and telephone numbers and some directories do not give more than the editors' and advertisement managers' names. Others give a complete breakdown of specialist editors and correspondents. Some of these are updated on a quarterly rather than a yearly basis. They are more expensive than the others but they do enable you to keep your lists up to date.

Most of the directories listed below should be available in the reference section of your local library, but after an initial study at the library it is advisable to buy one or two for company use. They will be needed not only to compile the initial list but also for reference purposes.

The Blue Book of British Broadcasting: standard reference book of TV and radio national and regional broadcasting stations, their programmes, presenters, producers and executives.
Telex Monitors Ltd, 47 Gray's Inn Road, London WC2X 8PR

Television and Radio Annual: a guide to independent TV and local radio.
IBA, 70 Brompton Road, London SW3 1EY

PR Planners UK and Media Selection Guide: lists the names, position and telephone numbers of key media contacts, TV, radio and press. The media selection guide is biannual and the *PR Planner* produces provisional bulletins which are issued every three weeks and complete revision supplements every six weeks. There is also a European version of the *PR Planner* which gives special reference to trade and technical publications.
Media Information Ltd, Hale House, 290–296 Green Lane, London N13 5TP

Pims Media Directory and *Pims Unique Townslist:* The media directory lists editorial contacts in the UK media. It is updated monthly. The townslist is a town-by-town guide to regional and local electronic and print media.
4 St John's Place, London EC1M 4AH

Editors: editorial information in a number of volumes updated monthly.
London Information News Distribution Agency, 164–166 North Gower Street, London NW1 2ND

IPC Business Press Information Services Ltd, East Grinstead, Sussex

British Rate and Data (BRAD): this is the directory used by media advertisers; it includes audience and readership profiles as well as audience and circulation figures.
76 Oxford Street, London W1N 0HH

Benns Press Directory: there are UK and world versions

of this directory. Information includes the names of specialist editors on the national daily papers. Otherwise information is limited to the editors' and advertising managers' names.

Union House, Eridge Road, Tunbridge Wells, Kent TN4 8HF

Willings Press Guide: this directory includes a fairly comprehensive foreign directory together with a guide to the UK media. Information given is similar to that in *Benns Press Directory.*

Windsor Court, East Grinstead House, East Grinstead, West Sussex RH19 1XA

World Press Encyclopaedia
UK Distributors: Mansell Publishing Ltd, 6 All Saints Street, London N1 9RL

Overseas Media Guide
Overseas Press and Media Association, 122 Shaftesbury Avenue, London W1V 8HA

Foreign Press Association in London: List of members.
11 Carlton House Terrace, London SW1Y 5AJ

Guild of Agricultural Journalists Year Book: lists specialist writers in this field.
Goldfield Mill House, Miswell Lane, Tring, Hertfordshire HP23 4EV

Guild of Motoring Writers Year Book: lists specialist writers in this field.
Fairfield, Pyrford Woods, Woking, Surrey GU22 8QT

Who's Who in Financial Journalism
4 Broad Street Place, London EC2M 7HE

Also worth looking at to keep up to date are the *Radio Times* and *TV Times:* useful sources of information on current programmes together with the names of the presenters and producers.

Advance Magazine: this publication lists details of forth-coming editorial features and supplements planned in the UK press. Contacts, copy dates and telephone numbers are given.
Longwood House, Datchet Road, Old Windsor, Berks SL4 2RQ

The NUJ Freelance Directory
314 Gray's Inn Road, London WC2

The choice

To complete the media list consider the following categories and make your own selection in the light of the analysis made of the uses to which the list will be put.

Television

This section takes in two BBC channels with 11 regional television stations, BBC Breakfast Television, and 16 independent television companies plus Channel 4 and TV-am.

News: In the UK the major news programmes are organised nationally by the BBC and ITN (Independent Television News). However, the independent television companies and the BBC regional centres also have their own newsrooms. Material which starts out at regional level may also go on to be used on the national networks.
Contacts: News editors, newsroom reporters and the BBC Future Events Unit at Broadcasting House

Diary and news magazine programmes: These too are organised both nationally and regionally by the BBC and networked by the independent companies. On the whole they are biased regionally.
Contacts: Editors, producers, reporters and researchers

General or women's interest magazine programmes: These may be regional or national.

Contacts: Editors, producers, reporters and researchers

Specialist series: These programmes are usually on for a limited period and cover specialist subjects such as holidays, motoring, food and wine or industry.
Contacts: Editors, producers, reporters and researchers

Documentary programmes: These are usually made by the TV companies themselves, but there have been occasions where the film has been made jointly with an outside organisation.
Contacts: Producers and editors

Discussion and panel programmes: These are usually concerned with an in-depth coverage of items of topical interest.
Contacts: Presenters and producers

Chat shows: These programmes can be useful when trying to build up a personality.
Contacts: Presenter, producer

Give-away and competition programmes: Many items are given away as prizes or at premium prices, and while these are not named by brand an item which is immediately recognisable can acquire some useful exposure.
Contact: Producer

Props for drama and serial sets: Sets have to be dressed with contemporary articles and some products can very usefully be supplied to studio property rooms.
Contacts: Producers or studio property room managers

For most of these programmes there is more than one possible contact and each of these contacts has its advantages. The editor is in charge of policy and content and the producer is responsible for putting the programme together. Both of these people may be too senior for a discussion on props, but they have the most influence and you might be able to interest them in an idea for future use. (Incidentally, by editor I mean programme or news editor. Don't confuse him with the film or videotape editor, who cannot help you!)

The reporters are useful contacts but they are often difficult to reach. Researchers are the people who gather suitable material for inclusion in a programme and are probably the most approachable people on the production team. However, they do not have the final say on what is included or on what is rejected.

Radio

This section takes in four BBC channels with 11 regional stations and more than 20 local stations plus IRN and more than 35 independent local stations.

News: Radio news coverage, like television news, is organised nationally by the BBC and IRN (Independent Radio News). However, the four BBC national stations broadcast their own news bulletins and it is advisable to contact the newsrooms for these programmes separately.

The BBC local radio stations and the independent stations may also have their own newsrooms and broadcast their own local news programmes in addition to the national news.

Contacts: News editors and newsroom reporters

News magazine, discussion programmes and phone-ins: These usually include live interviews with people who feature in the news or who are able to provide some in-depth information on both topical and general interest subjects.

Contacts: Producers, editors, reporters and researchers

Specialist series: These programmes are similar to the specialist programmes on TV.

Contacts: Editors, producers, reporters and researchers

Musical chat shows: This type of programme fills the majority of the time on local radio. The programmes are always on the look-out for live or taped interviews.
Contacts: Producers, presenters and researchers

Newspapers

This section might take in EEC newspapers, or indeed the newspapers of any country with which your organisation trades as well as the UK press.

National daily newspapers: This category comprises those newspapers which are published from Monday through to Saturday. They are usually printed overnight, though the first editions for distribution in the most distant areas of their circulation will be run in the late evening, with new editions coming out as necessary until around 4.00 am. This means that little material is of any use after the late afternoon and all the background material will have been written earlier in the day or the day before. Feature material may be written even earlier. It is worth remembering that most editorial staff will not be in the office much before 10.00 or 11.00 am.
Contacts: News editors and news desk reporters, picture editors, specialist editors and correspondents

Sunday newspapers: Most Sunday newspapers in the UK have a national circulation, but there are a few regional ones as well as 'national' Scottish and Northern Ireland Sundays. Some of the national Sunday papers include magazine sections, which are edited quite separately from the newspapers themselves.

There is far less news in the Sunday newspapers and much more feature material. This means that they require more notice of events and happenings of interest than the daily papers. Remember not to contact Sunday newspaper journalists on Monday – they will be having their weekend break!
Contacts: News editors and news desk reporters, picture editors, specialist editors and correspondents

Regional or city daily newspapers: There are around 100 regional papers in the UK, which is unique in having both these and national dailies. In other countries, such as the US where distances are so great, there are no national dailies but only regional or provincial papers. Some of the UK regional papers appear on the bookstand first thing in the morning and, like the nationals, they are usually printed in the late evening or overnight, so the same considerations apply to the timing of the supply of information.

In addition to the morning papers, there are also a substantial number of evening newspapers. The term 'evening' can sometimes be something of a misnomer, as some of them publish their first editions mid-morning. Material will need to be sent in very early in the morning to catch the first edition!

Contacts: News editors and news desk reporters, photographic editors, specialist editors and correspondents.

Local weekly newspapers: Most towns and the suburbs of large cities have their own weekly newspapers. The news and feature material is heavily locally oriented, with little in the way of national news except as it affects the local area. The newspaper will often be 'put to bed' the day before the publication date, so that material should be in by then.

In some heavily populated areas there are separate editions of the weekly paper with different titles for neighbouring communities. These series carry pages which are common to all editions and other pages which are aimed only at the small circulation areas. Other local papers cover quite large areas with a single edition, while yet others are circulated to specific ethnic groups. This means that local weekly papers vary tremendously in the size of their circulation and therefore in the size of their income and their staff.

An increasing number of weekly newspapers are issued as free sheets and are delivered door-to-door free of charge. Their editorial content is usually limited to items of consumer interest and the editorial staff is kept to a minimum. They can be very useful outlets for PR material.

Contacts: (Depending on the paper) editors, news and features editors, specialist writers and local reporters.

Press agencies and wire services: There are a number of press agencies based in London and in the provinces who cover news events and feed their material to the national and other papers. The Press Association supply the UK press with home news and newspapers subscribe to their wire service. Material sent to them should not exceed 100 words.

Reuters deal with financial material generally and the foreign press. There are also other news agencies which specialise in the reporting of news and the supplying of features to the press.

Contacts: News editors and news desk reporters, specialist editors and correspondents

Foreign press: There are scores of London offices of foreign newspapers. Alternatively the material can be translated and sent direct.

Contacts: London correspondents or the relevant editor or correspondent *in situ*. Another method of reaching foreign media is via the Central Office of Information, a UK government agency based in London.

Magazines

This section may include specialist magazines published in the EEC or in any country with which your organisation deals. There are so many magazines in this section that it is impossible to list all the categories. Here are the broad outlines.

Consumer magazines: These magazines cover all kinds of popular subject such as motoring, gardening, photography and sports, but by far the largest group is women's magazines.

Each of these groups of magazines can be broken

down into smaller groups depending on the audience at which they are aimed and the degree of specialisation of their contents. Specific motoring magazines, for example, may cover general motoring, motor racing, particular brands of cars, motoring holidays, car mechanics, second-hand cars and many more subjects.

They can also be classified by frequency. Some are published weekly, others monthly and yet others bi-monthly or quarterly, and the 'lead times' or periods between material being received and appearing in the magazine can vary from three or four days to six months or more – an important point to bear in mind when planning a press campaign.

Contacts: Depending on size, the editor, specialist editors and reporters and researchers

Trade, technical and professional magazines: There are even more magazines in this group than in the consumer group and it is safe to say that whatever the trade, profession or industry there will be a publication to deal with it. In some instances there may be a good many more than one, but here again the magazines will specialise in a specific area and a good deal of study is required to make sure that a particular magazine will be able to use the material you are planning to send to it.

Never underestimate the power of the trade press. The 'Grummit-Maker and Tube Weekly' may not have the glamour of a national daily, but the opinion or recommendation of the editor of the former could actually bring business to your company. Trade editors are often asked for their opinion of an organisation or for the names of suppliers, and if the relevant editors know your company well it could be your company which gets the recommendations.

Contacts: The editor, news and features editors and reporters

Local magazines: Most regions have their own glossy magazines and some also have more newsy and less glossy magazines produced either by independent publishers or by local authorities or community groups. They are usually looking for good material of local interest. Contact: The editor or reporters

Freelance writers: A good deal of the material written for the magazine press and to a lesser extent for newspapers is produced by freelance writers. These people can be difficult to track down, but they do tend to specialise in specific subjects. Study the specialist magazines relevant to your organisation and check on the authors of outstanding feature material. In this way a good freelance list can be gradually built up.

Teletext and electronic systems

Both the BBC and the independent broadcasting companies offer teletext information systems, Ceefax and Oracle, which are available to viewers with special sets. Most of the information on these one-way systems is aimed at the consumer or private viewer rather than firms or businesses. Viewers can get timetables, menus, programme information and so on.

Rather more sophisticated is British Telecom's Prestel service. This is a two-way system using telephone lines; users can conduct a 'conversation' with the Prestel computer. As well as being able to select from an even wider range of information, Prestel customers can actually make bookings and have them confirmed and will, increasingly, be able to buy a wide range of goods and services using their credit cards to pay.

Busineses which are Prestel information providers will be able to supply information on their products not only to the general public but also to select groups within a particular business or profession. Travel agents, for example, already use the Prestel service extensively.

What to include on your list

Any mailing list must obviously include the name of the TV or radio station or of the publication and the address.

But, of course, this on its own is not enough. A news release sent to *The Times*, New Printing House Square, Gray's Inn Road, London WC1 may possibly find its way to the one person who will be interested in it, but it is not very likely.

The addition of the words 'The Editor' are still not going to solve the problem, since the editor of a national newspaper is hardly likely to be interested in the launch of a new kettle or the fact that your organisation has discovered a new way to process cheese! The mailing list therefore must include the position of the relevant editor or correspondent, such as the Home Editor or the Industrial Correspondent. It should also include that person's name. This final requirement makes it far more difficult to keep the list up to date but experience has shown that a personalised approach is much more successful than a plain 'to the industrial correspondent'. The personalised method ensures that the material will reach the right person. It also tends to indicate that the PRO is taking some care with his work and is not just sending out material on the off-chance that it might interest someone. If you do not have a directory which includes specialist editors' names a quick phone call will soon elicit the information.

Incidentally, it is also useful to have a list of relevant phone numbers. This might not need to be quite as comprehensive as the full mailing list, but it will save time looking up numbers when they are needed as part of the ongoing media relations programme.

How to organise the list

Once you have been through the various categories listed above and picked out all the names to be included the next step is to arrange them in some sort of order. One way of categorising the names is to list them by the type of medium in much the same way as they are listed in the media guides.

However, some of the sections, such as the consumer and trade magazines, will need to be broken down still further into more useful groups. Thus if the plan is to send out a release on a new range of products the most useful sections can be immediately picked out of the list. Here are some examples taken from a variety of different fields.

Sample section headings for the mailing list of a food manufacturer

National daily and Sunday news editors
National daily and Sunday newspaper financial editors
National daily and Sunday newspaper marketing correspondents
National daily and Sunday newspaper technical and industrial editors
National daily and Sunday newspaper cookery writers
National and regional TV and radio news editors
National and regional TV and radio food and cookery programme compilers, producers and presenters
Local radio stations
Regional daily newspaper financial editors
Daily and weekly newspapers: news and industrial editors of papers near to factories and offices
Regional daily newspaper feature editor or cookery writers (possibly a weekly list as well)
Women's interest and home interest magazines, split into sections
Food and cookery magazines (consumer)
Camping, caravanning and holiday magazines
Health and vegetarian magazines
Catering industry publications
Retail trade and grocery magazines
Butchery and food trade magazines
Nutrition magazines
Food manufacturers and processing magazines
Marketing magazines
Consumerism publications
Financial publications

From time to time other sections may be needed but lists can be made up as and when they are required for specific projects.

Thus for the launch of a new range of soups the specific mailing list would include the following groups:

Consumer material:	National and regional TV and radio food and cookery presenters
	National daily and Sunday newspaper cookery writers
	Local radio stations
	Regional daily (and weekly) newspaper features editor and cookery writers
	Women's and home interest magazines
	Food and cookery magazines
	Camping, caravanning and holiday magazines
	Freelances in the field
Trade or specialised material:	National daily and Sunday newspaper marketing correspondents
	Marketing magazines
	Retail trade and grocery magazines
	Food manufacturing and processing magazines
	Butchers and food trade magazines
	Catering industry publications
	Freelances in the field

However, the list would be very much shorter for a story about a small new extension to one of the production units enabling greater production of some lines. Such a list would include the following sections:

Daily and weekly newspapers local to the factory

Local radio station
Food manufacturing and processing magazines
Retail trade and grocery magazines
Butchery and food trade magazines
Freelances in the field

In neither case will the material necessarily be sent to every publication listed within the sections chosen. This is the time for an individual assessment of whether or not the material will be of interest to the particular magazine and its readership. The name of any publication which will not obviously be interested in the material should be omitted from the list for this particular mailing.

Sample section headings for the mailing list of a heavy goods vehicle manufacturer

National and regional TV and radio news editors
National and regional TV documentary producers
National daily and Sunday newspaper news editors
National daily and Sunday newspaper transport editors
    and correspondents
National daily and Sunday newspaper financial editors
Regional daily newspaper transport and industrial editor
Regional daily and weekly newspaper editor and repor-
    ters of those papers near to plant and offices
Heavy goods vehicle magazines
Transport and freight publications
Motor trade press
Agricultural and farming publications
Army publications
Civil engineering magazines
Engineering publications
Public works press
Municipal and local government press

The precise choice of trade and industrial publication groups will depend upon the types of vehicles manufactured by the company.

Sample section headings for a small company producing highly specialised photographic equipment cleaning materials

National and regional daily newspaper technical and industrial editors
Cleaning and maintenance press
Commercial photographers' publications
Consumer photographic magazines
Printers' and photosetters' publications
Regional daily and weekly papers near to the factory and offices

This is obviously a highly specialised list and some care would need to be taken to find out exactly which publications are ever likely to cover the subject and who on these publications will be the most useful contact.

Checklist for compiling a media list

1 Define target audiences against agreed objectives and list the types of medium that reach these audiences.

2 List newsworthy activities which are likely to occur with reasonable frequency and key interested media into the above list to give an integrated list of possible types of outlet.

3 Invest in one or two good media guides for compilation and reference purposes.

4 Check through all the possible categories of TV, radio and the press and make up a classified list of specific editors, producers, correspondents and reporters who are likely to be interested in the material you plan to send out.

5 Ensure that the list includes names, addresses, telephone numbers and lead times.

The mechanics of the media lists

The most newsworthy and well-written release will not achieve any coverage if it is sent to the wrong outlet. Nor will it do any good if it is sent to the right outlet at the wrong time. This means that in an ideal world a new mailing list has to be compiled for each story or piece of information you want to impart to the media.

There is no problem here if the information is very specialised and only likely to be useful to a few outlets. If on the other hand you frequently send out stories which will be of interest to quite a wide selection of the media it will take too long to go through a large directory and jot down the names every time.

In-house lists

One answer is to compile a comprehensive media list, as outlined above, which takes in all the groups which are likely to be contacted with any frequency. When a story is ready to go out the executive will be able to pick out those categories which are relevant to the material and then go through these sections to handpick those journalists who will really be able to use material.

Such a list may quite simply be typed out on sheets of paper and duplicated so that additions and changes may be made until the list has to be retyped for clarity's sake. It can include telephone and telex numbers and lead times as well as names, positions and addresses. Envelopes or labels are typed each time a story goes out. This unsophisticated system will probably work very well if there are not too many large mailings over the year. But it will be very time-consuming for secretarial staff if there are a great many.

A slightly more sophisticated system is to put the names, positions and addresses on stencils or to use an addressograph system. Telephone numbers can be kept separately, on a card index or in a contact book. The stencils can be run onto sheets of labels every time there is a release to go out, or envelopes can be prepared in advance, sorted into those for dailies, weeklies and monthlies, and stored for future use.

The disadvantage of the latter system is that there is a tendency to stuff all the envelopes in a section with the material simply because it is easier than going through them all, and because the gaps will have to be made up or envelopes wasted if only a few are to left out of one section.

For PR departments which have invested in, or have access to, a word processor or small computer, the problem is solved. The media list can be stored on disk. The release or letter will be typed and edited on the word processor and distributed to the relevant sections of the media list. As more and more organisations go electronic, so will the material be able to be transmitted electronically to the media. Once there it may appear on the editor's data bank visual display unit as a single-line headline. If he is interested he will be able to view the first paragraph to see if the material will be of interest to his viewers or readers. If the material is not felt to be strong enough it can then be erased. The editor may never read the rest of the release. This look into the relatively near future highlights the importance of writing media releases in such a way as to catch an editor's attention at once. (See Chapter 3 on how to write releases.)

The problem with all ongoing lists is that they are liable to be out of date almost from the day they are compiled. Changes in media personnel are fairly frequent and nothing gives a worse impression of the PR executive than the continual receipt of material with a predecessor's name or even their predecessor's predecessor's name on it   The constant updating of all media contacts should be of top priority and should not be put off and put off until a spare moment arrives. If you have not been in contact with someone for some time and do not have a directory which is updated frequently, a quick phone call will tell you whether your contact is still there or has moved on. Indeed the information about his or her new position could be almost as useful as the name of the new incumbent of the old job.

The most usual method of sending out information to more than a few broadcasting stations or publications is by post. However, the information could be of immediate interest and if so either telex, Intelpost or hand delivery will need to be considered. Some messenger services or mail bike companies will do runs based on a supplied mailing list at so much per address and such a service might be used for rushing material to the offices of national daily newspapers. Failing such a service an executive or senior secretary in a cab can do the job equally well.

Media release delivery services

An alternative method of distribution is to use one of the agencies which specialise in the delivery of media releases. These include:

> London Information News Distribution Agency
> PIMS (London) Ltd
> PNA Services Ltd
> Universal News Services

The last of these is a news wire distribution service which sends out PR material to those newspapers which subscribe to the service.

All these agencies make sending out mailings much easier but they can be very expensive, and unless you give very precise and detailed instructions about which journalists in each category of the media should receive the release you may still be sending to media which cannot use the story. This is a waste of money as well as annoying to the media concerned.

Some agencies offer special services which can be useful for specific jobs. PNA Services, for example, offer a regional weekly newspaper distributor service which goes to 700 publications for quite a modest fee. EIBIS

International offer a translation and foreign distribution service for releases and photographs. They will also place technical features overseas on a nationally exclusive basis.

Personal contacts

A great deal of emphasis tends to be put on personal contacts, as though knowing a journalist personally somehow puts him or her in your pocket. Nothing could be further from the truth.

Provided that your material is newsworthy and you ensure that it lands on the right person's desk at the right time, the chances are that it will be published. Many thousands of stories, large and small, and even feature material are placed with no more than a press release in the mail or some short telephone contact, and even PROs who work regularly with their own trade publications may, because of the distance between their offices and those of the publication, never have met the editors.

It is often assumed that personal contacts will push through more of your material than that of other PROs and that you will be able to ask for favourable comment here and there. In practice, most journalists judge all the material that comes to them on its merits, whatever the source. The fact that you have enjoyed a few jars together will not cloud a journalist's judgement. And if a journalist is able to do you any kind of legitimate favour he or she will certainly feel that you owe him or her one in return; this debt may be called in when you are least able to be informative.

Too close a contact with leading journalists could be of more benefit to the media than it is to you. It is often very tempting, after a pint or more, to tell your journalist friend a secret or two 'off the record' or to air your grievances about the organisation for which you work. For both your sakes keep everything 'on the record' or keep your mouth shut.

However, if you need to work particularly closely with

specialist or local media it does make sense to get to know the organisations and their needs, and meetings with editors and journalists to see how you can best help each other are a good idea. These kinds of contact are easy to make for they are of benefit to both sides. A telephone call explaining why you want to meet will usually be sufficient. The sort of relationship you will be seeking to establish is rather like the one you have with good business colleagues.

On other occasions you may want to place specific feature material or to say 'thank you', and personal meetings are obviously useful here. For more on this aspect of media contact see Chapter 6.

Summary of Chapter 2

1   Define objectives, target audiences and activities for which a media list will be used.
2   Compile a general list of media which are likely to be contacted frequently during a normal year.
3   A specific list can be prepared from this list every time information needs to be sent out.
4   Decide how the material can best be stored.
5   Alternatively check on the services of outside media release distribution houses.
6   Work out a routine for updating the media list on a regular basis.
7   Decide in which area personal contacts will be of most use and make contact by telephone.

3 Releases and captions

The media or press release is one of the basic communication tools of any media relations programme. It will be needed almost every time you have any information to give to the media. Changes in company policy, new products and services, financial results, staff appointments, sponsorship news, factory openings – in fact almost any 'happening' or change within your company or organisation will probably merit a release to at least a few papers or radio stations.

In an ideal world each news outlet would receive a release tailored to its particular needs, and indeed this is sometimes possible. But more often the numbers are such that one or perhaps a small number of different releases are duplicated and sent out by post or by telex to media selected from the lists detailed in Chapter 2.

Releases will also be needed at any kind of event to which the media are invited, whether it is a top-level news conference, an exhibition press briefing or a sponsored sporting event. Where appropriate, photographs illustrating the content of the release will also be needed; unless it is purely a photo-story these must be captioned separately to the release.

How to write a good release

The vast majority of written material sent to the media ends up in the waste-bin – some of it unread; this despite modern training in PR and the many courses which are now available. All too often releases are written to please the management of the company rather than to fulfil the requirements of the media.

Most editors have become disillusioned with material which comes to them from PR sources. Comments in a personal mini-survey ranged from 'I'm fed up with reading endless puffs for "me too" products' to 'why can't these people take our readership into account?'

The highest percentage of useful material I could find any editor to admit to was around 25 per cent and some quite literally stated that they did not bother with PR material at all. There really is no excuse for this state of affairs when it is quite easy to write a good straightforward media release.

Content

Whatever the subject of the release there are a number of simple questions to which the editor or journalist needs to have the answers. They are:

> Who?
> What?
> When?
> Where?
> Why?

If at all possible, answer these questions in the first sentence of the release or at least in the first paragraph. Each answer can then be elaborated in the following paragraphs in order of importance.

This method of constructing a release enables the editor to assess the importance of the story at a glance. It also means that it can be subbed to fit the available space without any rewriting. It is unlikely that editors will bother to rewrite the relatively small stories which are the bread-and-butter material of most media relations programmes. It also means that if the piece is cut you, or rather your company, will still benefit from having all the facts reported albeit briefly.

Here is a sample release, which refers to an event to launch a government-sponsored industrial development scheme.

MINISTER LAUNCHES FIRST ENGLISH DEVELOPMENT ZONE
Tadchester New Town determined to attract new industry and cut unemployment

The Rt. Hon. John Smith, Minister For Industry, today [date] cut through a symbolic piece of red tape at Tadchester New Town to mark the launch of the very first English Development Zone.

The Minister welcomed the initiative already shown by the Tadchester Industrial Development Centre in attracting five new companies and 600 jobs to the area in the first four weeks of the scheme.

Tadchester New Town is situated in the heart of the industrial midlands and has suffered major closures and a job loss of over 6,000 in the last three years. By selecting Tadchester as one of the new Development Zones the government plans to encourage new industry in the area.

The Zone covers 300 acres which, for the next twelve years, will offer unprecedented benefits for industrialists and investors. These benefits include rate-free privileges and industrial building allowances against tax, while planning procedures and red tape will be kept to a minimum.

The Development Zone scheme was announced by the government in May of this year. There will eventually be 10 zones in all, each of them designated in an area of particularly high unemployment. The government wants to stimulate new industry in these areas both by encouraging the growth and development of new companies and by the expansion of existing companies.

In addition to the benefits conferred by Development Zone status, Tadchester has a good deal to offer the industrialist. Geographically it is at the centre of many markets and its origins as a New Town mean that there are excellent housing and recreation facilities. It can also offer a workforce which through experience is willing, adaptable and ready to retrain.

ENDS

An analysis of this release shows that:

The first paragraph answers the relevant questions.

Who: The Minister for Industry
What: Cuts symbolic red tape
When: Today
Where: Tadchester New Town
Why: To launch the first English Development
      Zone

The second paragraph reports the Minister's comments.
The third and fourth paragraphs expand on the Tadchester Development Zone.
The fifth paragraph briefly outlines the Development Zone Scheme.
The sixth paragraph returns to the subject of the Tadchester Development Zone and gives more information.

Obviously all these sections could be expanded more, but this short release gives the facts.

In contrast here is a sample of the type of release which is definitely not appreciated.

SLIMMERS AHOY!

Good news for slimmers. Here's an end to worrying about totting up the calories in food and wondering whether you are eating the right thing. Brand A will do it for you. Brand A is an innovative product concept which will make life very much easier for all slimmers.

XYZ Foods have spent over a year researching and developing the product and they are convinced that it will answer a real need in the market. Many diets fail because they do not provide the variety of foods that the body craves and after a couple of enthusiastic days the willpower begins to weaken. Brand A has been carefully put together to ensure that the slimmer enjoys a wide range of textures and flavours and still has the psychological satisfaction of preparing the food he or she eats.

This wonderful new slimming aid includes three meals a day and there is enough for four days. All the slimmer needs to do is to eat the delicious contents with a slice of bread and some milk.

Brand A provides a really easy way of losing a few extra pounds of weight. The slimmer doesn't have to guess the amount of food eaten because it is all weighed out and there is no temptation to have one extra mouthful and so ruin the chances of successful weight loss.

There are three brightly coloured boxes in the pack and these can be eaten each day. Each day's meals have been put together by nutritional experts to provide the right foods in the right proportion and this includes proteins, fats, fibre, vitamins and minerals.

Brand A makes no claim on the amount of weight loss – because each individual is different, most people can expect to lose weight. It contains no drugs or appetite depressants. Just good straightforward nourishment.

Breakfast is made up of cereals, milk and an orange drink. Lunch is a choice of milk drinks and supper consists of a three-course meal of soup, savoury snack with bread and a dessert. This is so similar to the normal meal that no stigma is attached to the slimmer.
ENDS

This horror is only a slightly exaggerated version of a real release. The first paragraph tells the reader nothing at all – Brand A might be anything. Indeed the nature of Brand A takes some digging out of the mass of wordage. The information is given in no particular order and the copy is confused. Exaggerated claims and puffs appear throughout the text. There is plenty of irrelevant verbiage but no information on XYZ Foods, on prices or on stockists. The latter is particularly important for a national magazine. They do not want hundreds of readers' letters complaining that the product cannot be obtained in Manchester, when the release could have stated that the product was on test market in London and the South-East.

Here is a slightly shorter but much more informative version of the same release:

NEW FOUR-DAY SLIMMING PACK LAUNCHED
BY
XYZ FOODS

XYZ Foods today [date] launched a completely new slimming product called Brand A, which gives a calorie-controlled food intake for slimmers over a four-day period. The new product offers slimmers an easy way of ensuring that they do not exceed their daily calorie target. The pack will be sold, price £x, through chemists, department stores and some supermarkets.

Brand A is made up of four packs each containing a full day's food. All the slimmer has to do is to add a daily allocation of skimmed milk and a slice of wholemeal bread. The packs have been formulated to give as wide a variety of texture and flavour as possible.

Breakfast each day consists of high fibre cereals with skimmed milk and a Vitamin C enriched orange drink. For lunch there is a choice of flavoured milk drinks. Dinner or supper consists of three courses; soup, a savoury snack with wholemeal bread and a choice of flavoured desserts.

XYZ Foods are well-known for their pioneering work in the field of slimming foods and they have been researching this pack for the last year. The daily meals have all been specially worked out by trained nutritionists to ensure that they provide all the nutrients essential to a balanced diet. There are no drugs or appetite suppressants in the pack.

Because every individual is different XYZ Foods do not make specific claims about the amount of weight loss to expect, but most people will lose three pounds or more. The appeal of Brand A is that it does all the work for the slimmer. There is no worry about eating the right foods or exceeding the calorie target. For four days the slimmer knows that all he or she has consumed at the end of each day is the 1,000 calories contained in the meals.

Brand A is available, price £x, from the following chains. It will also be on sale in local chemists and department stores.
ENDS

The first paragraph answers the relevant questions:

Who: XYZ Foods
What: A new slimming product called Brand A
When: Today
Where: Chemists, department stores and super-markets
Why: The product provides slimmers with an easy way of controlling their calorie intake

The second and third paragraphs develop information on the products.
The fourth paragraph identifies XYZ Foods and reinforces their, and hence their product's, credibility.
The fifth paragraph develops the question Why and gives the justification for the new product.
The sixth paragraph reiterates the price and availability facts.

Generally releases should be short, sharp and to the point. This is particularly important if the release is going out on telex. But even if it isn't, it is far better to start with a concise piece of information which can be built up into a bigger story if the circumstances are right than to send out a wordy release which is immediately discarded.

Headlines

The headline for your release must seize the attention, which probably means that it should be short. But if possible it should also be a summary, in miniature, of the information you are trying to convey in the release. If this is not possible in a single short headline you can always add a second headline to give a little more information.
Of course you could try a tantalising headline but do remember that in the first instance you have to attract the attention and interest of the journalist or editor, who is not going to be tempted quite as easily as the reader might be. They have seen it all before.
Sometimes the most interesting or unusual fact in the story can be pressed into service in the headline. For instance 'Chocolate-coated Bees Gain in UK Popularity'

could attract attention for a general survey on sweet-eating habits in the UK; or 'Stamping Machine Breaks the Million Barrier' could stimulate interest in a release on a new piece of machinery.

Media requirements

Of course particular media may have different requirements, but on the whole the basic release as outlined above will be suitable for most of them. However, there are a few points which it might be useful to bear in mind when writing the initial material.

TV and radio:
Here the material will be used in the spoken rather than written form and you may want to rephrase the information accordingly.
News desks:
Whether working in TV, radio or daily newspapers, news editors deal in immediacy. Material should be very short and to the point. It should also be very topical. Advance information is particularly useful.
Specialist producers and editors and magazines:
Lead times, even for writers on national dailies, are longer in this area and there is more room for lengthier explanations provided they are relevant to the recipient's speciality.
Local media:
Regional dailies, weeklies and magazines and local TV and radio stations are particularly interested in their own area, so make sure there is a local angle to your story.

Angling the contents

The basic release is useful but it is *basic*. If time and budget are limited the release may have to do everything and indeed it can be usefully sent to all the media which might be interested in the story. But it is much more satisfactory to angle the basic release to suit the readership or audiences of the various media groups.

It is quite easy to do this by rearranging the who, what, when, where and why elements of the release and giving more emphasis to some of them than others. A new product release, for example, might be angled for the consumer media along the lines of the second release given above for Brand A. But for the retail trade press much more emphasis will need to be given to discounts, special promotions and advertising – in fact, full details of what's in it for the retailer. The opening paragraph might look something like this:

XYZ FOODS BACK NEW SLIMMING PRODUCT A WITH £1M LAUNCH PROGRAMME

XYZ Foods today [date] announced a £1m campaign to back their new slimming product Brand A. The product, which provides a four-day calorie-controlled diet for slimmers, will be offered to the trade at a special discount (full details attached) and will be backed by national TV advertising, point-of-sale material and a consumer competition.

Similarly material aimed at the technical and manufacturing press will need to carry details of the nutritional formulation and research, the manufacture of the food-stuffs and filling and packaging details.

Very often the consumer media tend to be thought of together as all one group, but this leads all too soon to the sort of comments outlined in the introduction to this chapter. The easiest form of discrimination is to cut out all those outlets and publications which will obviously not be interested. It will after all be a waste of time to send details of a luxury fur to a down-market magazine aimed at working mums and equally useless to send details of a white flour and additive-based convenience product to a health food magazine.

This is a good start, but there will still be quite considerable differences within the remaining group and it is worth checking to see if you can usefully angle your basic release to fit at least some of these requirements. Regional media, for example, will be looking for a connection with their area, magazines concerned particularly with healthy living will be on the look-out for any health angle and teenage publications will want to know the relevance to young people.

The chances are of course that you will not have time to go into so much detail, but you can use different headlines to highlight specific aspects of the story, and if you are aware of the requirements of each type of magazine you will at least be able to include back-up material which is relevant to their subject and readership and to follow up with ideas for more in-depth coverage.

Style

This is always a difficult area, as each writer tends to have his or her own style, which on the whole just gives variety. However, a clear and concise style is easy to read; floweriness or effusion is not. Avoid long words when simple ones will do. Remember that all the publication's readers may not have the command of language that you have.

The subject matter and the medium towards which the release is aimed are perhaps the two most important areas to think about. The *Financial Times* Technical Page editor, for example, will not appreciate a very chatty approach, whereas teenage magazine editors may well be looking for a little modern slang with which their readers might identify.

A little humour or chattiness often helps to enliven a rather dull subject, but both humour and a chatty approach are often associated with the fact that there is no real content to the story, so don't overdo it. Quotes are also a useful tool – not yours, but those of a satisfied customer, of the person concerned or an expert in the field.

Editors also object to overblown or false claims. Don't say the product is unique if it is only another 'me too' product and don't say it's new if it is only the packaging which has changed. This wastes the journalist's time.

The PR person is very often in a cleft stick between how he knows the media will react to his story and the sometimes almost mindless enthusiasm of his client or boss. The journalist sees new products coming through all the time, and though some of them represent a real breakthrough in their field most are not really very exciting. The marketing man on the other hand is full of enthusiasm for this latest onslaught on the market and most certainly does not think his new 'baby' is at all routine. All too often the PRO writes the release to please the marketing man and the fulsome description may actually mask an important fact which would have interested journalists on the receiving end.

Another common complaint from editors is about the release which gives the impression, perhaps without actually saying so, that the product or service is a new one. The journalist spends time on the story and then discovers that the subject has been around for years. If the story has gone through to printing the PRO's stock will be even lower and he should not expect very good coverage in the future.

It goes without saying that downright lies are just stupid. They are always discovered and the end result is extremely bad relations.

One or two practical points should also be considered under style. Spellings, titles, and the use of initials in place of long names are all very important. Always double check releases for the correct spellings of names, places and addresses, brands, lists, ingredients and the like. Get titles right as well and if you are using initials for long names always spell out the name at least once.

Back-up material

The sensible use of back-up material provides an opportunity to be really selective in the material sent to particular media.

Provided that the main release is concise and to the point, editors are usually quite happy to receive background material which is relevant to the interests of their readerships. Indeed some editors of specialist columns and journals tell me that they like to receive good background material so that they can keep it to use as a reference for future articles.

Others need the extra information to answer readers' letters, whose numbers in some instances can be quite substantial. Those dealing with the replies do not want to have to keep getting on the phone to the PROs concerned.

Background material for the Development Zone release outlined earlier might include the full text of the Minister's speech, the government leaflet setting out details of the Development Zone scheme, a complete list of the benefits to be gained by businesses from setting up in Tadchester, and a list of addresses of relevant officials within the local council, the New Towns Commission and Tadchester Industrial Development Centre who might be able to help industrialists to take the decision to move.

If time permitted, separate releases might also be written on the firms which had already agreed to go to Tadchester. The industrial writers on the nationals and the relevant trade and technical press would be the target media here.

The slimming product's back-up material might include a complete nutritional breakdown of the contents of the pack and some research material showing how often slimmers stray from their diets. If distribution was limited a list of stockists could also be useful.

Checklist for writing releases

1 Is the release short and to the point? If appropriate, develop important points in the back-up material.

2 Does the headline attract attention and tell a story?

3 Does the release answer the questions the editors will want to ask?

Checklist: continued

4   Is the release relevant to the readership of the media for which it is intended? 5   Check spelling, prices, stockists and the like. 6   Cut out all padding, puffs and hyperbole.

How to write a good caption

Very often releases are accompanied by photographs and these can be very important. After all, an editor can always write up the copy himself but he cannot so easily produce a photograph. They are also particularly important for small specialist magazines who rely heavily on photographs supplied from outside sources. Other media, of course, may not require photographs at all, and more of this will be found in Chapter 4.

However, if photographs are to be sent out they must be captioned. This may sound obvious, but it is surprising how many editors say they are for ever clearing out photographs which have no identification. A good picture tells a story, says the old newspaper adage, but unless the recipient is psychic it will at least need the name of people and products filling in.

Like releases, captions should be kept short and to the point and unless the picture is going out as a photo-story with no separate release, this means very short indeed.

A photograph taken to accompany the release on the Tadchester Development Zone might show the Minister cutting the red tape with the various local officals looking on. A short caption might read:

> *Caption*
> The Rt. Hon. John Smith, Minister for Industry, today [date] cuts the 'last piece of red tape in Tadchester' to launch the first English Development Zone in that town. He is watched by (left to right)

Councillor James Jones, Leader of Tadchester District Council, Mr Alan Peters, Director of Industry for Tadchester, and Councillor Bill Taylor, Chairman of the Council.
ENDS

This caption reflects the who, what, when, where and why questions important for good releases:

Who – everyone is identified by his position and actions and full names and titles are given.
What – Cutting the 'last piece of red tape'
When – Today
Where – Tadchester
Why – To launch the new English Enterprise Zone

Here again it is very important to ensure that all names and titles are spelt correctly. Product shots, too, must have everything in the picture fully identified.

I recently received a photograph of what looked like a measuring jug with a spout like a teapot rather than with a lip at the top. The caption ran as follows:

Caption
No more worries about making gravy, no more worries about the cholesterol levels and no more worries about spillages. The X Brand Super-Jug solves all these problems and many more.
ENDS

I was not much wiser after reading the caption than I was before. Here's a better attempt at a caption for the same picture.

Caption
The X Brand Super-Jug pours gravy from the base of the jug rather than the top, thus leaving the fat in the jug. The Super-Jug is manufactured by ABC Plastics Ltd and is on sale now price £1.20 in hardware and department stores all over the country.
ENDS

This caption tells you:
  Who – ABC Plastics Ltd
  What – A new gravy jug
  When – Now
  Where – National distribution
  Why – Allows you to pour gravy without getting all
      the fat on the plate too.

Checklist for writing captions

1   Is the caption short and to the point?

2   Does it identify everyone or everything in the picture?

3   Double check all the spellings.

The mechanics of the release

The paper for the release, its layout and the sign-off information can be almost as important as the release itself. The good impression created by the writing of a first-class release will soon be dissipated if there is no contact for further information, no space for print marks or subbing and no indication that the release has ended and that there are no more continuation sheets.

The paper

The quality of the paper is partially dictated by the fact that it must be suitable for the various duplication processes used to run off large numbers of the release. It must also be robust enough to withstand the wear and tear of the postal system and the editor's desk. However, a really heavy paper does not impress and is often seen more as ostentation than as a sign of quality.

The letter heading on the paper should be easy to read and should carry identification of the company issuing the release, together with its address, telephone and telex numbers. This sometimes leads to problems if the PR is being handled by an outside consultancy. Some PR firms send out releases on their own letter-headed paper, which can cause confusion. In other instances the client company insist on using their own letter heading or at least a brand identification. In practice the latter method is preferred by most journalists because they can see from whom the information originally came. However, it is also important to make sure that the journalist knows who and where contacts are; more of this later.

Most media release paper is designed to attract attention and if this is not overdone it is a sensible idea. Journalists who are working regularly in a certain field will come to know the look of your paper and this can be very useful.

Many companies identify release paper by the words PRESS RELEASE or NEWS RELEASE. Strictly speaking the former ought to Read MEDIA RELEASE – important, perhaps, if you send a good deal of material to TV and radio. The words 'News Release' also have a pitfall in that much of the material you will be sending out will not actually constitute hard news. To overcome this point some companies print special paper for feature material sent out on a regular basis. Examples are fact sheets, recipes and research material.

Captions can be typed on shorter pieces of headed paper, but more often they are typed on plain paper or labels and stuck to the back of the photograph. See pages 58-9 below.

Contact information

It is extremely important to give full details of the people who can be contacted for further information, and this, of course, is in addition to the company or organisation's name and address printed on the release paper.

Details of relevant contacts are usually typed on the last page of the release as follows:

For further information contact:
Judy Ridgway,
Ridgway PR Ltd
Tel: 000 0000 Eves: 000 0000

Ann Williams
XYZ Foods
Tel: 000 0000

Here details are given both of the executive at the PR consultancy working on the account and the relevant executive at the client company. Very often PR consultancies only give their own executives' names, but there are times when a journalist will want to 'go straight to the horse's mouth' and a contact within the client company can be very important.

The details also give a home number to contact at the evenings and weekends – essential if the story is likely to have any national significance. If a story is really important two contacts are also very useful. All this information must also be included on captions, and if plain paper is being used the address should be added.

Layout

The release must be set out in such a way that it is easy for the journalist to use it. A story of marginal interest may make it simply because it was quite easy to sub, whereas another similar story is spiked because the lines were too close together and the margins were very narrow.

Here's a checklist of layout points to watch:

The margins: Wide enough for print marks and subbing
Double spacing: Leaves space for print marks and subbing
Typed on one side only: Allows for cutting out and pasting up
Underlining: Never underline in a release as this is a printing instruction to set in italics
Capital letters: Use these only for proper names and for a few dignitaries such as Her Majesty the Queen, Prime Minister, Archbishop and Field Marshal. Managing director or chairman does not rate capitals. Do not use stops between initials such as CAM or UNO

Numbers: Numbers should usually be spelt out one to nine and at the beginning of a sentence. However, figures are retained for dates, addresses and prices.

Carry over: Try not to carry part of a sentence over to the next page and if at all possible leave paragraphs intact as well.

Page identification: Every page should be numbered and should carry a continuation note at the base of each page and at the top of the next. This makes any pages loss quite obvious and also means that the material always stays in the correct order.

The words 'for immediate release' are superfluous. Why else did you send the release out?

Ending: The word END or ENDS can be typed at the end of the copy before the contact details, but it is not really necessary if the contact details are there.

Dates

All material sent to the media should be dated, with the precise date, not just June 1984 or May 1980. The date has an obvious value if the story is a topical one but it also helps the journalist to check how long he or she has held the material.

If the material is not topical and is delayed for some time before being sent out the date should be changed. In the past I have come across complaints from editors that they have received old material. This can cause problems on the news desk and does not create a very good impression.

Embargoes

Occasionally the nature of a story is such that it must not be released before a certain date. This is not too difficult if there are only a few media outlets involved and if their lead times to publication are the same. However, it could be that you want to send the same information to TV, radio, national dailies, the local evening paper and the weekly trade journals. If so an embargo can be employed to make sure that the material is not published before a certain time. In essence an embargo is a request not to publish before the date and time stated. It is usually set out as follows:

Embargo: 12.00 noon, Monday, 21 January 1984

Embargoes should be used only if they are really necessary and a good deal of the embargoed material which reaches an editor's desk does not really need this form of restriction. The excessive use of embargoes devalues the practice and makes it more difficult to ensure that the embargo is kept when it is really important.

Captions

Never write directly on the back of a photograph. It will probably show through. Always use some kind of paper or label. There are various schools of thought on how captions or short photo-stories should be affixed to photographs. One fairly popular method is to type the caption on an A4 sheet. This is then stuck to the back of the photograph with sticky tape and folded over to protect the front of the picture.

The second method uses a smaller sheet of paper or a large label which is then gummed to the back of the photograph. With this method the caption cannot be easily removed, which from one point of view is a benefit since the picture will not easily lose its identification. On the other hand the journalist cannot simply mark up the caption for printing; it will have to be retyped. With the first method the picture is all too easily separated from its caption and becomes one of the candidates for the waste-bin mentioned earlier.

A sensible compromise is to use the first method for longer photo-stories and to add a sticky label to the photograph giving outline details and the source and to use the second method for short captions.

Always type the word 'caption' at the top of the page. If the caption does become detached the finder can see at a glance what it is. It is just as important to ensure that the contact names, addresses and phone numbers are included on captions as on releases. Some PROs seem to forget this.

Envelopes

The main consideration with envelopes is that they should be large enough and strong enough to accommodate the material to be contained within them. Always use hard-backed envelopes when sending out photographs and if possible use stickers or type in the words 'PHOTOGRAPHS. DO NOT BEND'. This helps to discourage postmen from forcing fragile material through small letterboxes.

Delivery

The vast majority of releases are sent out by post. However, other methods such as telex, Intelpost or hand delivery must be used for really urgent material. The news desks of national dailies, for example, and radio and TV need to have news the same day. After that it ceases to be news!

The strategy of the release

All too often there is no strategic planning behind the use of media releases. Something happens within the company and the decision is taken to send out a release. The release is written and sent out in a blanket mailing of all the media outlets on the PR department 'Press List' and the PR sits back and thinks the job well done. But to be really effective the mailing should have had a good deal more planning behind it than this.

Is the release really necessary?

This is the very first question which must be asked and the answer will lie in the content of the information to be imparted and the media which might be interested.

Sometimes the answer to the question is 'Yes, but only for a handful of specialist writers or magazines'. If this is the case it might be much more effective to scrap the mailing and to talk personally to the journalists concerned. There could then be a real opportunity to give each one an exclusive angle. One major multinational even uses this method to communicate details of its financial results. This type of communication is covered in more detail in Chapter 6.

On other occasions the news to be imparted will be of great interest to a variety of media and a full-scale mailing will be required.

Sadly the answer 'No' is rarely given to this question and because of this a great many releases go out which are of marginal interest to the recipients. The reason often lies in an over-eager management who are continually hounding the PRO for more column inches or to keep up with the supposed coverage of competitors. These people only feel happy if they are approving press releases at regular intervals.

The far-sighted and strong-minded PRO will not give in to such pressures and will try to explain the pitfalls of such a course to the powers that be. Naturally even he will want to see the maximum level of coverage achieved, but the method is not mass mailings but the sort of activity outlined in Chapter 10.

Planning the mailing

Once the decision has been taken to go ahead a good mailing should be planned under the following headings.

The mailing list

Ideally PROs should check every name on the complete list and take a decision on whether or not each person will really be interested in the release. However, this may not always be possible and a good list will be categorised in such a way that sections can be taken out and used as appropriate.

The content of the release

Does the release need to be angled differently for the different sections of the list? Or will it be sufficient to include background material as appropriate?

Photographs

Are these really necessary and do all the sections of the list need to have them? Photographs can be expensive both to produce and to mail. Radio, of course, cannot use pictures – a fact often overlooked by zealous PROs! Some publications like to take their own shots and others are not illustrated. A list of available photographs could be included with the mailing for all but the certainties.

Timing

This can be one of the most important considerations of the strategic plan. Media vary in their frequency of publication, some appearing every day and others only at bi-monthly intervals. Radio and TV can react even more quickly than daily newspapers, with an item going on air only an hour or so after it has been received.

The lead times for the many publications on your media list can vary tremendously, some monthly magazines having a lead time of six months or more. There is not much point, in these circumstances, in sending the material out all at the same time. By the time the monthly magazines come to publish, the news value of the story will have completely disappeared and the story, if it is a good one, may have been worked to death. No journalist will thank you for this.

Thus if you want the news to break at roughly the same time the material will have to be sent out at intervals appropriate to the lead times of the publications concerned, and there is always the risk that the nationals will hear of the item and decide to publish it. Embargoes can be used but only in really important cases.

Orchestrating publication can also be difficult because

of internal factors. New product launches, for example, are often sprung on the PR department long after the lead times for important monthlies and weeklies have passed. On other occasions the project is a secret one, though in this instance key media can be taken into your confidence, in advance.

Follow-up

Another regular complaint from journalists is that the PROs concerned are never in their offices the day after they have sent out an important mailing. This may be a bit of an exaggeration but where it is true much damage is done. So do make sure that at least one of the contacts listed at the foot of the release is around to answer questions.

It is also sensible to plan a follow-up campaign with key media. The strategic use of background material which has not been sent to any other media and an appropriate idea or two can achieve an in-depth feature which would not otherwise have been forthcoming.

Summary of Chapter 3

1   Write releases and captions to suit the needs of the media rather than the sometimes inflated ideas of management.
2   Answer the questions that the journalist will need to ask in the first paragraph of the release and develop the various points in order of importance.
3   Write in a concise manner with no padding, puffs or hyperbole.
4   Check all spellings, titles etc. in both releases and captions.
5   Use specially designed release paper and lay out the release with regard to subbing requirements.
6   Make sure that at least one and preferably two contact names are given at the foot of the release and the caption

together with phone numbers for both day and night.
7 Question the validity of the release and if it is
worthwhile plan the mailing in detail.

4 Photographs

Photographs can be almost as important as news releases. A good picture is worth any number of words for it can communicate a point quickly and succinctly, and in any language. Editors like pictures and many a mediocre press release has found a place because it was accompanied by an eye-catching or interesting picture.

However, adding photographs just for the sake of it is not a good idea. Photography is extremely expensive and should only be undertaken if it is necessary – which is not the same as being marginally useful or pleasant. There are, of course, occasions when photographs are taken to please the chief executive or for company records. This is all very well in its way, but do not make the mistake of thinking that the media will also be interested; unless the picture tells a real story they will not be.

The true value of a picture lies in its ability to illustrate a point or to act as an eye-catcher both to the editor and subsequently to the reader. If the same picture can achieve both purposes then so much the better. A PR executive faced with the task of showing the strength of steel-capped safety footwear hired a double decker bus and had it photographed as it drove over the feet of a man wearing the boots. He certainly made his point! Another successful bus picture was taken by the sponsor of a fleet of painted buses from London, Birmingham and Manchester. The buses were offered to a leading charity to take deprived children on a trip to Woburn Safari Park. The buses were photographed with a few surprised giraffes looking in the windows. All the parties concerned gained publicity which they would probably not have achieved otherwise.

Sometimes, of course, the subject is either so technical or so complicated that a photograph of the laboratories or of a piece of machinery would not make the point and the use of drawings should be considered instead. Nevertheless there are few editors who do not like to use at least one or two photographs and the relevant drawings might be backed up with shots of the inventor or the experimental staff at work. It is sensible, however, to check with editors of really specialist publications whether or not they can use a good picture.

What to photograph

What you should photograph depends entirely on editors' requirements. Study the publications on your specialist media lists and get to know what sort of pictures are likely to be used.

Photography at special events

A very effective way to achieve publicity for a new factory opening, an exhibition, a fashion show, a lunch or a conference is to issue a general invitation to photographic agencies and to the picture editors of the daily press. Such an invitation should give an indication of what pictures could be taken or which parts of the event lend themselves to photographs. There may be innovative processes at the factory, new products on display at the exhibition and new designs at the fashion show. A lunch or conference may feature well-known personalities and speeches may be made which will be of interest to the media.

Once you have issued the invitation it is important to make sure that the photographers will be able to do their job. Space must be left so that they get an uninterrupted view, extra lighting may need to be laid on and someone must be on hand to make sure the photograph has an accurate caption. Some freelances have been known to leave without getting a full caption. You may also need to lay on a messenger service to deliver the film to the newspaper building while the photographer goes on to his next assignment.

You should also arrange to take your own photographs of this type of event, for they give you an opportunity to show off the newsworthy aspects of your organisation. Most of the publications which are likely to be interested in using pictures like these do not use colour photographs, so there is no point in wasting money taking them. The only exceptions are shots for television or for the Sunday colour magazines; unless these have been specifically arranged there is not much point in worrying about them.

Photography for general news stories

News of the day-to-day happenings within the organisation can be communicated with much more interest by photography. Examples include the installation of new plant, moving an unusual load or shipping fridges to Iceland, the chief executive leaving on a trip to China, long service presentations and involvement in local community activities.

As for special event photography black and white will be quite sufficient. An exception might be if your local paper is one of those that sometimes use colour on their pages.

Product photography

This can be one of the trickiest areas of photography, for very often the product is not really very different from many others on the market and what differences there are may be difficult to illustrate photographically. So before going ahead with photography stand back and assess whether editors will really be able to use the picture you are planning.

If you do decide to go ahead, there are a number of ways in which the product might be photographed. It can be photographed on its own or in a likely setting. It can be photographed in its packaging if it has any, it can be photographed in use or it can be photographed in an unusual setting. Depending on which publications you believe will be interested, you may need to photograph the product in two or three of these ways. The consumer press, for example, will not be interested in any kind of pack shot and brand and company names should be removed or kept very small indeed. There are some newspapers which simply will not use a picture if it has any brand identification whatsoever.

Shots of the product in use or in an unusual setting are the type to aim for in this area. But do not get too carried away with the idea of a gimmicky photograph. It may just make one of the down-market dailies and thus please the marketing director, but it is probably not going to sell very much of the product. Such a photograph is more likely to help sell the newspapers! On the other hand there may be publications on your media list which will be interested in showing the packaging, particularly if it has any unusual features or uses new techniques. Retail publications, too, are more likely to be interested in close-ups of the product itself or in the promotional and publicity material which will help them to sell it.

Photography for feature material

For certain types of consumer product it can be very useful to have a selection of photographs which can be placed with supporting feature material. Food products are an excellent example. Very often the packaging is too heavily branded to be able to use a straight pack shot and a picture of a plate of soup or a bowl of cornflakes is not going to stun the readership! However, if these items are made up into attractive dishes they can be photographed and used to good effect with features on 'Supper Dishes with Soup' or 'Crunchy Toppings'. Some of this work should be in black and white for use in regional media and certain magazines, but the majority will need to be in colour.

For economic reasons many consumer magazines are increasing their use of outside photographs. Sometimes these are commissioned for specific features following an approach from the PRO. Others have been taken 'on spec' and placed with suitable magazines at a later date.

Beauty features highlight another problem which can arise if the parent company is based abroad. The parent company, perhaps in France or in the USA, will probably have taken a portfolio of beauty pictures when the products were initially launched in their home country. Very often they expect UK PROs to use the same photographs in their own press campaigns. This rarely works. The models look indefinably 'foreign' and unless the feature is on French or US fashion the pictures will not be accepted by the UK press. A new set of pictures will have to be shot.

Checklist for photographs

1   Decide if a photograph is needed. Will it be able to tell the story better than the release?

2   Make a list of those media to which the picture will be relevant, showing black and white or colour requirements.

3   On the basis of this list decide what exactly should be photographed and how it should be presented.

Choosing a photographer

Photography is a highly specialised business and apart from the odd record shot it is not usually a good idea for the PRO to take his or her own photographs. For one thing there are usually very many other things at an event which need to be organised and directed by the PRO and a well briefed photographer can take at least one burden off the PRO's shoulders.

For product and feature work it is even more important to have a professional. Photographers are trained to get the best out of models and to arrange the lighting to the most dramatic effect, and they are usually very creative as well. Photographers' fees are, of course, quite high and there can also be a problem choosing photographers for events outside the area in which you normally operate. In these circumstances a PRO who has a good camera and who knows what he is doing may decide to take publicity shots of local events and newsworthy items such as new employees, new sports facilities or retirement presentations. Remember, though, that this is not the end of the story. The pictures have to be developed and printed to a suitable quality for the media and you will need enlargements, possibly in some quantity.

Some large companies employ their own photographers but very often these people are expected to handle a good deal of clerical work as well as take and process all the photography. Some of them are very good indeed but it is unlikely that they will have been given the opportunity to develop skills in such highly specialised areas as industrial photography, beauty photography or still life.

Most PR executives will need to build up a repertoire of photographers who are skilled in the various areas covered by the media relations programme. A good industrial photographer will not be particularly good at portrait work and a fashion photographer will probably not know how to handle food, so if all these areas are represented by the activities of your company or client organisation you will need to find photographers in each field.

The number of photographers you work with in each field will depend upon the volume of work that you have and your personal relationships with the photographers concerned. It is sensible, however, to work with at least two and possibly three different photographers in any one field. This cuts down the risk of a photographer becoming stale and running out of ideas about how to present the material. It also means that if one photographer you know and like is booked up the other one will probably be free to work with you.

Sources of photographers

Register of Professional Photographers and Buyers Guide: The listings in this register are classified by county and town and an indication is given of the type of work carried out.
The Institute of Incorporated Photographers, Amwell End, Ware, Herts SG12 9HN.

Freelance Photographers List: This list is compiled by the Freelance Branch of the NUJ. Listings contain details of the type of work carried out by the photographer.
National Union of Journalists, Freelance Branch, 314 Gray's Inn Road, London WC1 8DP.

The Institute of Journalists also has a list of freelance photographers.
Bedford Chambers, Covent Garden, London WC2 8HA.

Other sources include the Yellow Pages of the telephone directory and of the *Hollis Annual* and groups of photographers such as that organised by Bill Hennessy Associates, Universal Pictorial Press and Picture Agency and Norman Edward Associates.

How to select a photographer

Always arrange to see some sample work when choosing photographers for specialist work, and if possible have a talk with the photographers in person. You may also want to see the studio and check on any special facilities which might be needed, such as access for large items, a working kitchen or space to build room sets.

This kind of assessment may be difficult if you are looking for a photographer at the other end of the country. Here a telephone conversation will usually have to suffice. But do keep records. It may be very useful to know that there is a first-class industrial photographer in Tyneside or that such and such a photographer near the Exeter depot should not be used again. If the job is very important it may be worth the cost of sending some one whose work you know well to cover the assignment. This may cost more at the time but could save a good deal of money in the long run.

The quality of the photographer's work is not the only factor which you may need to check on. It could be that one first-class photographer takes very much longer on studio work than another or that another industrial photographer cannot work without bringing in extensive lighting systems. There will be occasions when a slight loss of quality, provided that it is not too great, will be offset by budget gains or less disruption on the production line. The only way to find out this sort of information, short of using the photographer once, is to talk to other people who have used him or her. If you see samples of the photographer's work you will be able to contact the clients who commissioned the work.

Checklist for choosing a photographer

1   Does the photographer specialise in the area in which you need to commission photography?

2   Have you seen examples of his or her work?

Checklist: continued

> 3   Are you sure that the chosen photographer's
>   working methods will be suitable for the job in
>   hand?

Choosing models and other specialists

It is very rarely sufficient just to put the product on the
table and expect the photographer to get on with
photographing it. The photographer may very well have
sensible suggestions for backdrops and for simple accessories, but very often rather more is required.

It may be that the product would be shown off to best
advantage in use. This means that a decision must be
taken on whether the in-use setting can be re-created in
the studio or whether the photography should be done
on location. It also involves the use of models.

Models

With highly specialised products the models will probably be people who are already working with the
product. Professional models do not always look very
convincing in a factory or a highly technical laboratory.

If you are using 'real' people, make sure that they will
be reasonably comfortable in front of the camera. Some
people freeze up and look completely false. The only way
to check is actually to point a camera at the people
chosen before the main session. Try to keep the pictures
looking as real as possible. Too many beautifully clean
and pressed white coats, for example, can look staged,
and best clothes are quite unbelievable at work.

More often the photographic session will be in the
studio and it will be virtually impossible to work with
people who are not professional models in these very
artificial circumstances. Professional models are trained
to look at ease and to be able to produce spontaneous-
looking smiles and expressions to order.

Not all models are the curvaceous female variety and

studio shots can be set up with less glamorous professional models where this is required. Models, like photographers, specialise in certain types of work and they usually have portfolios to show off how they look in a variety of poses. This specialisation can be quite important; there are good reasons why a model specialises in hair fashion photography rather than hands or feet. Indeed pretty hands can be one of the most difficult things for a PRO working in beauty to find. Most models work through photographic model agencies. Some of these also specialise in male models, children and so-called 'uglies', or the less glamorous type of model. There are also agencies for animal models. Check the telephone directory or *Hollis Annual* Yellow Pages or ask the photographer with whom you plan to work to recommend some agencies. The agency will send you either their complete portfolio or a suitable selection of models to fit your brief.

If at all possible interview all models with whom you have not previously worked. Some models can be a very disruptive influence in the studio, particularly if there is more than one model on the session. It also helps to brief the model in advance so that he or she is aware of what is involved and will bring the right selection of clothes or accessories. If you are using models a good deal keep a model book with notes on how each one has been used before, what they look particularly well in and any other relevant notes.

One final point: always make sure that all models complete the 'standard form for signature by models' devised by the Institute of Incorporated Photographers and the Institute of Practitioners in Advertising. This form of contract ensures that the model cannot suddenly start demanding repeat fees on a photograph which is widely used.

Beauticians, accessorisers and other specialists

For some types of shot models will do their own hair and make-up, but if you are acting for a manufacturer of hair preparations or beauty products you will probably need to use a hair stylist and a make-up artist. Remember that leading professionals in these fields must be credited in the captions. Do not try to save money by using really unknown or inexperienced people in these areas – the results can be disastrous.

For certain types of photograph, particularly those for feature use, you will need to think about the accessories you will use in the photograph. This may simply mean adding a flower, an attractively draped scarf or a glass of wine to the products to be photographed, but it may also mean creating a complete atmosphere. One product may be used in a feature on Italian cookery while another may be the dominant part of the decor for an elegant drawing room set and yet another may appear in a greenhouse. For all of these photographs quite a large number of accessories or props will be needed to create the desired effect.

Photographers who specialise in food or in room set photography will probably have a good selection of props. In addition quite a few manufacturers of household goods are willing to lend their products for use in photographs for non-competing items in return for suitable credits. Large shops and department stores will be equally helpful.

However, if you are trying to create a period shot or a specifically national look you may have to hire props. Sometimes the photographers will organise this for you, but if there are a large number of photographs to take then you should consider using a specialist photographic accessoriser whose job it is to provide a good selection of suitable props from which you and the photographer can choose on the spot.

This type of photography also calls for other specialists such as home economists to prepare and present the food in front of the camera, room set designers and model makers. All of these specialists must be chosen with care and with an eye to the particular skills required. Some home economists are excellent at cake decorations, for example, while others are better at all-round cookery or pastry work. If you have not worked in these fields before ask the advice of the photographers. They will have specialists with whom they like to work.

Setting up the picture

Briefing

To take really good pictures photographers need to be properly briefed. They are not mind readers and unless you explain, in some detail, what you are trying to achieve with a particular photograph they will not be able to do their best work. You might, for example, be photographing a tractor. A picture intended to show the pulling strength of the tractor will need to be quite different in composition from one designed to show the gradients which it is able to climb or the revolutionary design of a new gearbox.

Photographers also need to be informed of the printing process involved in the publications for which the picture is intended. Some processes do not reproduce pictures very well and the subject needs to be in bold relief without too much fussiness, whereas other processes are able to reproduce every detail. They also need to know the type of publication for which the picture is intended. The composition of a photograph for the 'Truck Drivers Weekly' would be quite different from that for *Science Today* or for *Vogue Magazine*.

Location photographs

For location work it is very helpful to the photographer to visit the site beforehand. A good photographer should, if necessary, be able to produce good pictures without a previous visit, but he or she will certainly produce better results if they have had time to look round and plan the most effective camera angles. Such a visit should involve talking to personnel to try and understand something of their jobs and to work out how best to tell the story in visual form. Any technical points should be discussed with the relevant experts to avoid any arguments about the pictures afterwards.

Obviously the plant or area manager should be alerted both to any pre-shooting visit and to the photographic session itself. He, too, needs to be briefed on the need for and the purpose of the photographs, for it is important to ensure his willing co-operation. Disruption of normal activities should be kept to a minimum. This is important not only in the interests of keeping production flowing but also in obtaining the most natural pictures of the operatives and staff involved.

However thorough the briefing, the PRO still needs to go on the shoot. Once briefed, the photographer should be left to compose the pictures himself and if he says something will not make a good picture his judgement should be accepted. But as the PRO you can smooth the way. You can also check the final picture before it is taken. Not all location photography is centred on plant, machinery or buildings. Quite a number of 'mug shots' or portraits will be needed as people join the company or move their positions within it. This can be a very tricky area as most people are self-conscious in front of the camera. It is the PRO's job to help relax the subject. You can also brief the photographer on any idiosyncrasies, on interests and on which parts of the person's job might lend themselves to photography. In this way it should be possible to obtain a much more interesting picture. Show the transport manager with one of his fleet of lorries or talking to a driver, the canteen manageress in the kitchen or the sales director at a briefing session.

Studio work

In the studio the conditions are, of course, rather different. There is usually less urgency, though the time factor cannot be ignored since studio time costs money. The photographer will be much more in charge here but he or she will still need a detailed briefing. If other specialists are involved, a general briefing meeting will ensure that everyone knows exactly what is required of them. The PRO should then let everyone get on with their jobs. A point to watch is the delivery of a product or material to the studio. Very often this will be coming from a different department, who should be alerted in good time. Check with the photographer that the material has been delivered a day or so before the appointed date. This gives you time to chase it up if there have been any hiccups.

Live interest

On location or in the studio some subjects are just not very interesting, and anything which can be used to add interest will be very helpful. Human or animal interests almost always improve a picture, but the subjects should be used in a way that is relevant and which helps to explain the subject. Children playing with toys, men putting up prefabricated house units, a family in a holiday resort or a woman using a knitting machine are all likely to enhance the original subject.

People in the picture should be concentrating on what they are doing. They should not just be standing or lying about looking decorative. A blonde in a bikini does not really enhance a jeep or a cuddly dog a power drill. Sometimes people are used to give an idea of scale. A man standing beside a combine harvester or an ear-ring photographed with a close-up of the head will help to convey the size of the object.

Last-minute checks

Always check the final composition before the photograph is taken and ask yourself the following questions:

1 Is the picture relevant to the story?
2 Is it self-evident what the subject is or does?
3 Does the picture tell the story without the need for a long caption?

The next step is to check the detail, and this will need a

little more experience. If the shot is to be sent out in black and white the colour must be ignored and the shot viewed in terms of tones of grey. This means that the sharply contrasting colours green and black will look just the same in the black and white print. It also means that the choice of background colour is vital. An experienced photographer should have pointed out these things but it is sensible to acquaint yourself with some basic knowledge. A black and white polaroid will also help!

Composition can also present many potential pitfalls. One highly experienced PRO tells the story of her first photographic foray. The product was discreetly set out towards the back with the label half turned away. The picture looked attractive and showed a new use for the product. The only trouble was that the photograph was so arranged that it would be very easy for a picture editor to crop the product out of the picture altogether!

Checklist for setting up the picture

1   Brief appropriate managers that the session is to take place and arrange for any special facilities or sample product.

2   Brief the photographer in detail on the purpose of the photograph and its destination. Visit the site if possible.

3   Brief any supporting specialists in a similar manner.

4   Look for relevant human interest angles and action in the photograph.

5   Take the photographer's advice on what will and what will not make a good picture.

6   Check any technical points in advance and if mistakes could be made make sure an expert is present.

Checklist: continued

---

7 Keep disruption to a minimum and try to keep any live models as relaxed as possible.

8 Make a final check on the photograph before it is taken to ensure that it will do its job. Does the picture show the subject off to best advantage?

If you are satisfied with the answers to these questions then go ahead and authorise the picture.

The mechanics of the picture

How many shots to take

The first point to consider is the number of shots which need to be taken. This will depend partly on the requirements of the interested publications and partly on technical consideration such as variations in lighting and the medium being used. If the subject of the photography is a new type of ballpoint pen, for example, at least two shots will be required, one for the retail trade press and one for the consumer press. The former could include attractive packaging or promotional material, but this would be quite unsuitable for the consumer press. Here a shot showing someone using the pen would be much more appropriate. If the PRO felt that a number of different editors were interested in such a picture he might decide to take two or three different shots: one perhaps with a child drawing or learning to write, another in an office setting and another in the home with a woman writing a shopping list.

If the photography is in black and white the photographer may be working with reels of film rather than with plates, in which case he will be able to take many more shots without inflating the price too much. But for some forms of still life, for example, and for colour work the photographer will be working with plates, which are expensive in themselves. These technical aspects of the shoot should be discussed with the photographer in advance and the decision may be made in the light of the budget as well as of the PR requirements, to put a specific limit on the number of shots.

What editors want

Quite apart from wanting pictures which will enhance the pages of their magazine and which will interest their readers, editors need pictures of the right size and printed on the right sort of paper.

Editors want sharp, well focused prints which are glossy but not glazed. They should not be too large; indeed some newspaper block-making equipment cannot deal with prints larger than 10″ × 8″. Half-plate pictures, if they are well cropped before being sent out, are equally acceptable. Pictures for television should be 10″ × 8″ matt, preferably in colour. For those publications which use colour, transparencies can usually be accepted from 33mm upwards, but it may help the magazine if plate sizes are agreed before the pictures are taken.

Topicality can be important here. Nothing irritates a daily newspaper picture editor more than an allegedly topical photograph sent to him by post. Pictures must be delivered by hand to these newspapers on the day that they are taken. If you think that there is a good chance of a daily newspaper using one of your pictures but don't feel that they are likely to send their own staff photographers, a phone call to the picture editor could arrange the delivery of exposed film immediately after the event.

Take care with the choice of prints. If the photographer has used a reel of film ask for a set of contact prints with the photographer's own choice of two or three of the pictures enlarged. Check all the pictures and crop if necessary. Do not allow the photographer to stamp the back of the photograph. You are sending the picture out and are the contact for further information. Remember too that in times of industrial strife the photograph could be blacked if the photographer is not an NUJ member.

Sending out prints

All too often 50 or more prints are ordered from black and white photography and sent out indiscriminately to complete sections of the media list. Some PROs have even been known to send pictures out to radio stations! This is usually extremely wasteful and it tends to reinforce the inefficient image of PR executives.

However, there are some occasions when sending a photograph to a radio station is not such a bad idea. It could make it much easier for the presenter to describe an unusual item, and here perhaps a sample of the article itself might make life even simpler. Photographs can also be used to arouse interest in an event which would not otherwise bestir the news editor to send a photographer. A good example comes from the PR agency for a hair preparation manufacturer. This company holds a national hair colouring competition every year with regional heats, and radio had shown little interest either in covering the event or in interviewing the winners. However, when shown pictures of the amazing results achieved by the winning entrants, most of the local radio stations near to the regional heats interviewed the regional winners.

Photographs should only be sent if you are absolutely sure that the recipients will be able to use them – even to the press. If only a small number of publications are involved and you are not sure about photographs, ring up and ask.

Some organisations print a sheet of miniature photographs so that editors may choose which, if any, they would like to have. This can be expensive and if a large mailing is going to regional newspapers, for example, it may be more sensible to reproduce one or two pictures on the release and invite editors to request prints, or simply state that photographs are available on demand.

Make sure that all pictures leaving the Press Office are properly captioned (see Chapter 3) and that they are well protected. Pack with cardboard or with hard-backed envelopes and make sure that there are no paper clips to pierce the prints and that the address is not written on top of them in ballpoint pen!

Checklist for sending out photographs

1   Decide the number of shots on the basis of the budget and the interested media.

2   Choose prints carefully and crop where necessary.

3   Have the photographs processed to the right size and on the right paper.

4   Take particular care to get the topical pictures to the daily media the same day.

5   Only send photographs to publications you are reasonably sure will want to print them. Offer photographs to other publications by phone or by stating on the release that photographs are available on request.

6   Take care to protect pictures in transit.

Copyright

Editors always assume that photographs from PR sources can be used free of charge, and any PR outfit which tries to charge for pictures is likely to get short shrift. However, this does mean that your organisation must own the copyright of all the pictures you send out.

When a photographer is commissioned by a PRO to take photographs, copyright in the negative belongs to the photographer and copyright in the prints belongs to the commissioner. Thus the two must always work together on this particular photograph. Sometimes the photographer will sell his negatives to the commissioner, but the fee will be a matter for negotiation. This may be necessary if negatives are needed abroad.

If the work is commissioned by a PR consultant, the copyright is his unless it has been arranged that it should be assigned to the client. If the work is carried out by a staff photographer in working hours the copyright belongs to his employers.

The copyright on photographs taken by press agencies belongs to them and they may well expect to sell the pictures to news or picture editors.

Photographic libraries

There exist, chiefly in London, a number of photographic libraries which will supply prints and transparencies on topical or historical subjects where exclusivity is not a requirement. They charge a fee for the use of their material. You are unlikely to be using their services for material to send out to the media, though they could be a useful source of illustrations for internal publications, but you may be able to place some of your material with them for use by other organisations. The Central Office of Information is another organisation which may well be able to use your photographs.

However, you are much more likely to have your own photographic library with reference shots of all plant and personnel and a collection of possible feature material. Too often this 'library' is a mound of photographs, some without captions, in a single folder or drawer. A secretary or executive has to plough through them all to fulfil every media request.

To be really useful the photographic library should be carefully organised by subject and the system should indicate the following:

1 The date the photograph was taken.
2 The photographer who holds the negative.
3 Availability in colour as well as black and white.
4 The copyright holder if different from the normal.
5 Brief caption details.
6 The current whereabouts of the picture if you are

expecting it to be returned, and a regular reminder procedure.

7   Any restrictions governing publication, such as the correct acknowledgement.

It is useful to hold at least two prints of all black and white negatives and to re-order as these are sent out, and to keep black and white and colour libraries separate. A photographic library needs constant updating. Pictures of the chairman ten years ago or the old plant before the renovations are only of interest for the company history and are definitely not for current use. So check from time to time whether pictures should be retaken rather than re-ordered.

Colour transparencies are expensive and extra care needs to be taken to ensure that they are not lost through carelessness or neglect. Every loan should be followed up after a certain period of time. Some companies insist that journalists or other borrowers should sign a form to say that they will be responsible for any photographs borrowed and that they will pay for it in the event that a photograph is lost or not returned before a certain date. This seems to be carrying things a little too far. A number of circumstances in which a transparency could be lost or damaged would be quite beyond the control of the borrower.

You will soon get to know those publications which are regular users of your transparencies, and provided the pictures usually come back safe and sound there is no need for such formal contracts. After all, your organisation is benefiting from the continuous exposure of its products.

Summary of Chapter 4

1   Decide whether or not a photograph is really needed or whether a drawing might not be better able to make the point.

2   Decide which media will be able to use the picture

and plan the content of the picture or pictures accordingly.

3   Choose a photographer who specialises in the type of photography you require.

4   Make sure that all the appropriate supporting models and specialists have also been booked.

5   Brief the photographer and any other specialists in detail.

6   For location shots make sure that the team have every facility on site and go with them to smooth the way. For studio work ensure that all the material has been delivered well in advance.

7   Use human interest, action, close-ups and interesting camera angles to sustain interest.

8   Assess each picture before it is taken to ensure that the picture is relevant and makes its point.

9   Ensure that photographs are processed in a manner which will suit editorial requirements.

10 Send pictures only to those editors who you are sure will want to print them. Send details of the pictures available to other editors.

11 Agree how the copyright will be split before commissioning the photographs.

12 Keep prints and transparencies in a well organised picture library.

13 Keep picture library records and pictures up to date and make sure you know the whereabouts of every valuable transparency.

5 Samples and giveaways

In general, there are only two legitimate reasons for giving items to members of the media. The first is to provide a sampling facility and the second is to draw attention to products which might otherwise be overlooked. There is also sometimes a case to be made for offering a present as a 'thank you'. It should, of course, go without saying that presents as bribes are at best ill advised. Honest journalists will be justifiably annoyed and there is no guarantee that those who do accept will actually produce a more favourable report than would otherwise have been the case.

If you do decide to offer items to the media, your organisation or client's own products are by far the best giveaways, for they enable the producer, journalist or researcher to try them out for themselves before featuring or writing about them. It also shows that you have confidence in the product. However, there are occasions when the product is either too expensive or too highly specialised to give away. In these instances loans or substitute gifts may be considered.

Samples

Who should receive them

Usually there is no point in offering samples to people who do not specialise in writing about your section of the market. However, if a particular journalist writes about another part of your range of products it might be tactically useful to send samples of an inexpensive new product, even though it is not in his area, simply to remind him of your existence and to jog his memory about the rest of the range. The fact that you realise that it is out of his area of interest but may be useful to him personally should be made clear in the covering note that goes with the sample.

How far this tactical use of samples is carried will depend on the cost of the item, the cost of distribution and the number of interested journalists. A greetings card company, for example, may include journalists from teenage magazines on their list for sample Christmas cards. These journalists probably won't be able to write about Christmas cards in their columns but they will be interested in the current range of fun notelets and notepaper. On the other hand, there would be no point at all in sending the same samples to agricultural journalists, who would never have any occasion to write about the company's products.

More often the problem is to limit the list of recipients, for it can be a costly business sending out fragile pottery or expensive jewellery. Indeed the whole question of when a product becomes too expensive to be offered as a sample is very difficult. Obviously something like a car could only be considered a bribe; on the other hand a vacuum cleaner, say, may be too expensive to give away in bulk but could certainly be offered for comparative testing. Cars, of course, are also offered for comparative testing but there is usually no question of the tester keeping the car at the end of the trial period, whereas the vacuum cleaner would not really be worth the manufacturer's while collecting. Smaller and less costly items such as pens, beauty products and food are much more obvious candidates for a more general distribution.

When to give them

The next question to consider is when to offer samples. The most useful timings are when a new product is launched and when products are changed or modernised. However, products which are known to be available on request may receive better ongoing coverage in the media simply because they are useful for photography.

If the product to be sampled is important enough to rate a press launch then this is the obvious time to organise the sampling. If the item is not too heavy or too expensive it can be given away as part of the press pack the journalists take away with them – but do remember to provide good strong carrier bags.

Sometimes the product or range of products is too heavy to carry easily. A very effective mailing of product samples was carried out after the launch of a number of new additions to a range of condiments plus repackaging of the whole range. The company had special display boxes made which would take the complete range and this was distributed to the homes of leading food writers and journalists. It was, of course, a very expensive operation but one which achieved the introduction of a complete range of products into the kitchens of those people whose sampling of the product would be the most valuable.

On other occasions the product to be launched is considered to be over the limit of what can be given away and one creative idea which has now been taken up by quite a number of manufacturers is to raffle a small number of the items or to organise an amusing competition which journalists attending the launch are invited to enter. The prize, of course, is the product which is being launched. This sort of idea can be a talking point as well as a source of genuine goodwill.

Of course, a full-scale press launch is not always the

most appropriate way to introduce the product to the media. Some companies opt for a simple mailing of information supported by the product samples, or the complete package may be personally delivered to selected media by the PR executives concerned.

This kind of approach can be very useful since it provides an opportunity for the media to ask questions and get direct answers on the spot, without having to spend valuable time away from the office. It also gives the PRO a chance to find out how he can best help that particular journalist, and the questions of background material, samples for photography or testing and in-depth features can all be raised.

With this kind of exercise the most appropriate media can be picked out and the PR effort concentrated where it is both most needed and most appreciated.

How to present them

Sometimes a creative approach can give added interest to the pack. An idea used by both a leading paint manufac-turer on the introduction of a new type of paint and a hair product manufacturer on the launch of a new shampoo and which could be adapted to quite a number of other fields was based on the headline 'Don't write about it until you've tried it.' In each case the pack included the tools needed to carry out the job; in the case of the paint, a paintbrush and a mug for brewing up and in the case of the shampoo a hair brush and comb set and a towel.

Other products are seasonal in nature and a mailing or delivery of samples can serve to draw the attention of magazines with short lead times to the current availability of the product. One federation of vegetable producers packed a small basket with all the ingredients for a seasonal recipe featuring their own vegetables and sent it off to leading cookery writers on the national and regional dailies. The response was excellent; quite a few regionals published the recipe itself and two or three of the writers on the nationals featured that vegetable in their own favourite recipes.

An important practical point to consider when sending out mailings of this kind is to decide exactly where to send the package. Very often the most appropriate person to receive the samples is not a full-time member of staff and even if they are, packages of this nature are very easily lost in a large newspaper building. Certainly, if the product has anything to do with the home environment it would be sensible to think about sending the gift to the home address of the journalist concerned. Ring up to get the addresses. Most publications will give you a number to ring even if they will not give an address, and once you have spoken to the potential recipients you should have no trouble in getting addresses – and a convenient time – to deliver.

Some products will benefit from being generally available for photography or for legitimate testing. Food products, cookware and tableware, decorating materials, stationery and the like do not receive very much coverage after their initial launch. However, if the PRO is arranging feature coverage or if it is known that they will be available for photography their PR lives will be extended.

It is true that some journalists are greedy and ask for rather more samples than they require, but this is not the norm and these people are soon sniffed out. It is then up to you to gauge their importance to you and to decide whether or not to comply with their demands. Most requests, however, are both genuine and reasonable.

Loans and purchases

If your product is such that it is normally only loaned out, this must be made clear at the start. Keep a note of the whereabouts of each item and institute a regular system for calling back and collecting items which have been loaned out. It is also worth working out a scale of charges which can be used if an author or editor asks to buy equipment which has been used in tests for a book or for a comparative feature. Of course, if the former is to refer exclusively to your product it would be a generous gesture to waive the return of the equipment.

Another scale of wholesale charges for unused equipment is also useful for people who like a particular product so much that they genuinely want to buy it for themselves, albeit at a preferential rate. A good deal of real embarrassment can be caused by simply giving an expensive item to a journalist who knew she would not be able to write about a product in any depth but expressed a wish to buy it. A wholesale buying facility can also be a very useful part of a factory visit or a fact-finding interview at head office.

Dispatch

If you are working as an in-house PRO it is usually quite easy to arrange to send sample products out from the factory or workshop. But if you are working from a consultancy or from an office situated at some distance from the manufacturing units you will need to organise a system for sending a product out and checking that it has gone. It is all too easy to take and agree to a request for samples, ring up the appropriate department or dispatch centre and happily assume that it has gone. Quite often it hasn't and even if it has it may be helpful to call the recipient with information on delivery and timing.

An alternative method is to have a stock of sample material in or near your own office. However, this, too, has its drawbacks. The product may be difficult to pack or it may need to be kept under refrigeration. If the merchandise is valuable and indeed even if it is not, there could also be a problem of pilferage.

Checklist for samples

1   Decide whether samples are really necessary and make a list of possible recipients, indicating prime targets for expensive items and tactical targets for inexpensive products.

Checklist: continued

> 2   Consider when samples should be made available: at the launch of a product, when changes are made or as part of the ongoing publicity back-up for a product.
>
> 3   Work out the mechanics of delivery.
>
> 4   Draw up systems to cover the storage, loan and possible return of items offered for testing or for photography.
>
> 5   Consider offering wholesale terms to members of the media.

Giveaways

There are a number of occasions when a gift other than the product might be considered. The product itself, for example, though useful may be so commonplace or so inexpensive that it has little intrinsic interest outside its own application. The launch of a new type of scouring pad, say, might suggest the gift of an oppropriately inscribed or patterned tea towel or a new range of pens the gift of a set of writing paper and envelopes.

On other occasions the product is just too expensive to give away. Alternatively it may be of great specialist interest to the readers of a particular set of publications but of no personal interest or use to the staff on those journals. Highly specialised manufacturing equipment, chemical cleanser for photographic equipment, or nuts and bolts for plumbing equipment do not readily lend themselves to sampling, but a case might be made for including small but appropriate gifts in any press pack.

Of course, there is no necessity to include a sample or a gift in any press pack and indeed simply including these items for the sake of it and without a clearly defined idea of why you are doing it is a waste of money. However, a really creative approach can be a great attention-fixer and have a lasting effect. The PR agency for a national group of citrus fruit growers sent out a tiny orange tree in a plant pot as part of the invitation to a press lunch on the subject. That plant is probably still sitting by the desks of a number of influential food writers offering a constant reminder that oranges make an excellent ingredient in all kinds of cooking.

There are all kinds of giveaway which could be used in place of product samples. But to be of any real use giveaways must be both useful or decorative and relevant to the product or service you are promoting. Before including them in any press pack the question 'Will this be of any use to the recipient?' must be answered in the affirmative. If it is not it will be a waste of time and money to include the gift and it may even be detrimental to your relationship with individual members of the media.

Christmas presents

Christmas presents should ideally be offered as 'thank you' gifts for mutual co-operation throughout the year. Product samples or items relevant to the product are the best choices and the item should not be too expensive. However, you are the only person who can judge the value of the relationship.

Christmas gifts are very much personal gifts in that there is no need to send them to everyone on your lists. Of course some companies do this and one or two manage to benefit from it by sending out a different type of product from their range each year. One international soup company managed to continue its corporate image-building campaign by sending as Christmas presents boxes of biscuits and chocolates made by its continental subsidiaries.

Interesting gifts have included pestles and mortars from a spice company, silver measures from a whisky company, small silk scarves from a cosmetics company, cuff links from an industrial diamond company and paper knives from a leading stationery company. The examples are endless, so if you decide that Christmas presents are appropriate for your operation all you have to do is use your imagination to find the right creative approach.

Summary of Chapter 5

1   Gifts or free samples should only be given to the media for sampling purposes, to draw attention to a new, changed or ongoing product, or to say 'thank you'.
2   The product itself is by far the best giveaway. However, the question of the value of the product should be looked at in some detail.
3   Only give samples to journalists who will actually be able to use the material gained.
4   Offer samples at the launch of a new product or when changes are made. They may form part of the press kit at a press launch or they may be mailed or delivered personally.
5   Consider the advantages of personal delivery.
6   Use samples to draw attention to seasonal variations and to products which are easy to overlook; consider a general offer of products for testing or for photography.
7   Draw up systems to cover storage, dispatch, the return of loans, sales or used products and wholesale prices.
8   Consider other forms of giveaway where products are unsuitable to offer as samples or gifts. Choose useful or decorative giveaways or ones which are appropriate to the product range and its uses. Will it seize and hold the attention?
9   Consider whether a Christmas present will be an appropriate 'thank you' for co-operation throughout the previous year.

6 On-going information service

An on-going media information service is very much the backbone of any media relations programme. It supports the publicity for important activities and launches and provides the day-to-day contact which is so essential in ensuring that the organisation and its activities, services and products receive a steady stream of coverage throughout the year.

Unfortunately this is the least glamorous of any of the activities of a busy public relations office and it tends to receive the least attention. Everyone is happy to jump-to and work hard on a new factory opening or a big product launch, but they are not so eager to rush off and fulfil the everyday requests which come in from the media. Yet service given to the media at this level can determine the outcome of much more important media decisions in the future.

Most editors and journalists are perfectly honest about the fact that when they need help they tend to go to those PROs who have been helpful in the past. A transparency sent round in a cab or a special piece of artwork produced at short notice can be just as valuable as an exciting launch or a slap-up lunch. Indeed it will probably contribute to a very much better relationship.

Nor is the role of an efficient information service purely a passive one. An imaginative PRO or press officer will be thinking up new and useful angles for in-depth feature material suitable for specific programmes or publications and will be spending a good proportion of his or her time selling them. Unfortunately, not enough thought is put into this area and many editors complain about the lack of creativity displayed in the ideas put to them.

Organising the service

The degree of formal organisation given to the media information service depends to some extent on the size of your organisation or, for a consultancy, on the size of the fee extracted from the client. Some large organisations have specially designated press officers working within a press office which, though coming under the surveillance of the public relations department, is separate from it. Other organisations designate a press officer within the PR office and others simply expect all the PR staff to act as press officers as the need arises.

It probably does not matter what title is held by the people who will be dealing with press enquiries, but what does matter is that they should be reasonably *au fait* with the company and its products. The lack of even basic knowledge is probably a fault encountered more when dealing with a consultancy than with in-house PROs. If the query is of a complicated or technical nature it is quite acceptable to pass it on to the expert, but is this really necessary for a bar of soap or a DIY fitting?

As well as having a good working knowledge of the subject with which you are dealing, you, as an efficient PRO, should also have at your fingertips the names and telephone numbers of people within the organisation who are competent to speak to the media on specialist subjects, and this list should include others apart from the brand managers and marketing department personnel. There is nothing more annoying to a journalist who is working on a story than to be told that the PRO will ring back with the relevant numbers and then not to get them for another two or three days.

If the queries coming into the public relations or press office are short questions they can usually be answered on the spot, but quite often they will be in the form of a general request for information on a specific topic and it could be that your organisation has in its files a good deal of material which could be sent out. Do make sure that all this material is filed in such a way that it is easy to find and is related to any photographic or other reference. Some information services are organised in such detail that they have a grandiose title such as 'The Barbed Wire Information Bureau', information sheets and a direct telephone line. However, such a detailed service is usually organised primarily for the consumer rather than for the media, though answering press queries will be part of its function.

If you do have a fairly sophisticated information service it is easy to think that you have all the answers to hand, but this may not be the case. So when taking down details of media enquiries don't just record them: listen, be constructive and ask questions. If you know what the story or feature is to be about and the angle from which the producer or journalist is approaching it you will be able to be much more helpful. There may be a booklet on the subject, a special expert in the technical department who has sat on the relevant government fact-finding commission or a market research survey giving the latest market trends, any of which would help the journalists far more than the standard handouts.

Telephone manners and service

Most journalists agree that the telephone manners of

some PR departments leave a good deal to be desired. Some of them leave the impression that they are really too busy to deal with media enquiries and unless the journalist can use the name of a well known programme or a national daily the service is grudging to say the least.

However, there are other PROs who are extremely friendly and helpful on the phone. This immediately puts their organisation in a good light and the journalist is disposed to feel that this outfit may be a useful source of information in the future.

If this friendly attitude is followed up with prompt service the good impression is stamped even deeper. Too often the executive forgets to phone back until the next day. Or even worse, the material promised does not arrive until the end of the following week. It has even been known for a company to respond to a request for information six weeks after the initial query and then to complain that their product had been left out! There also sometimes seems to be a feeling that the media could have got themselves better organised and asked for the material earlier. There is occasionally some truth in this, but very often the journalist's deadline is looming close, and the PRO is supposed to be providing a service not a favour.

Checklist for an efficient enquiries procedure

1 Be friendly and helpful throughout; do not give the impression that it is all too much trouble.

2 Record the details of the request and ask for further details about the proposed story so that you can dig out the most useful in-depth material. Indicate that this is the reason for your questions.

3 Drop everything and treat the request as extremely urgent. Even if you know that the answer can wait until the next day it is far better to deal with it at once. It may be forgotten later on.

Checklist: continued

---

4 If you need to phone back, do so as soon as possible. Phone back within twenty-four hours to report progress even if you do not yet have the answer.

5 If you leave a message for someone else to phone the journalist back, check to see that they have not missed the message or forgotten to fulfil it.

6 If the request is for an expensive sample use tact in discovering whether it has a genuine background. You may not have heard of the journalist or author concerned but that does not mean that they are not engaged on a bona fide testing programme or working on a first-class magazine feature.

7 Where necessary send material by cab or messenger.

8 Check to see that both postal or hand-delivered material has arrived and whether the journalist needs any more material.

Day-to-day contact

Getting the enquiries procedure right is only the first stage in setting up a good media relation programme. The second stage is the much more active one of going out and securing a steady stream of coverage for the company and its products or services. Start by making a list of the areas in which you think you might be able to generate coverage over a three-month period. Such a list of objectives for the PR department of a food manufacturer might look something like this.

1 Feature material on cooking with a variety of the products in women's magazines and in regional media.

2   A series of radio interviews on local radio.
3   A feature on the use of some of the products in pubs for a catering trade magazine.
4   An in-depth feature on the new soup production line in a leading food production magazine.
5   An in-depth feature on the work of the new product development team in a food technology publication.
6   A visit to the Peterborough factory – where new jobs are coming on line – by the industrial editor of one of the national newspapers.
7   A feature on the activities of the Skelmasdale factory social club in the local media and a possible visit by the local radio station disc jockey to a social evening.

And a similar list for a heavy goods vehicle manufacturers might look something like this:

1   A release on the year's export success for both the heavy goods vehicle publications and all the publications covering the industries to which the goods were sold.
2   An in-depth feature on the conversion of a standard line for use in a mountainous area for a leading magazine in the field of civil engineering and for publication in the country concerned.
3   An on-site demonstration of the current range of earth-diggers for publications covering public works and civil engineering generally.
4   A feature on the new managing director for the heavy freight publication.
5   A feature on safety aspects of carrying chemicals and other dangerous substances for a lorry drivers' magazine.

To achieve the list of objectives set you will need to be in constant contact with the leading publications in your field and in occasional contact with all the other publications which might be useful. This contact may be by post, by telephone or by personal meetings; the choice will depend very much on how important you are to a magazine and the magazine to you and thus how often you are likely to be working with this particular publication, how physically near you are to each other and indeed how well you get on at a social level.

However, if you have creative ideas and good material, face-to-face contact is by no means necessary. Unfortunately many editors feel that this kind of creativity is absent from the activities of a number of PROs. The only material they receive is the syndicated material which is sent out to everyone on the mailing list, and there is little attempt at placing original and exclusive material.

Syndication of material can work quite well at a regional level, though even here blanket coverage can be a real waste. If, for example, you are running a recipe or a beauty information service you will be able, over time, to build up a list of regional dailies and weeklies who use the material regularly. Some sophisticated services send out portfolios of material to selected users and these are updated from time to time. If the subject is one which is likely to be covered fairly regularly the expense of such an operation will be recouped. But for most products and service this sort of exercise would be too expensive. However, the success rate for syndicated material can also be increased by sending out material with themes which are relevant to the local area or which are topical.

For national media the approach must be rather different. Monthly mailings are no use at all, and ideas are needed in the first instance rather than completed material. Once you have sold an idea to an editor you can then discuss how much material you will supply and how much the magazine will want to write or photograph for itself. Some magazines are pleased if you can produce an illustrated feature to an agreed plan. Others have a large enough budget to be able to retain their independence, these publications will probably ask for background material only or will send a journalist to cover the story on the spot.

However, if you are to write the feature remember to check on the editor's requirements as to length, the number of illustrations, the date of issue of the article and the copy deadline. Sometimes it is worth thinking about getting a well known person in the field to write features for you or at least to suggest his or her name to the publication. This will be a more expensive way of producing feature material but it may also make it more acceptable.

If your work is mainly in the trade and industrial area it is even more important to keep in constant touch with the leading publications in the field. An editor will appreciate it if you supply him regularly with information about the company, giving him advance warning of changes and additions to the product range, the factory or indeed any aspect of the company's activities. A good relationship in this area can mean extra coverage since the editor will be more inclined to ring your company for quotes or for filler items. Editors have also been known to remind PROs that their exhibition details have not yet been received   Nor should you forget the media local to your offices and factories. Community relations can be extremely important but they are very often relegated to the bottom of the list of PR activities.

Checklist for active day-to-day contact

1   List areas which are likely to generate coverage during a set period.

2   Look at this list in terms of the relevant media and make a list of objectives to achieve within the period.

3   Send out syndicated material to specially selected regionals and place specific features ideas with nationals and specialist magazines. Be as original and creative as possible by letter or phone.

4   Once features have been placed take care to fulfil the editor's requirements.

Informal entertaining

Though entertaining is not an essential part of the media relations programme it can often help to smooth the way. Be discriminate in your entertaining. If you are taking a journalist to lunch you should know exactly why you are doing it and what you expect to achieve from it. Even more important, you should know what you have to offer. Journalists will not appreciate your wasting their time, however good the lunch.

Reasons for individual entertaining might include any of the following:

- Briefing editors or journalists on changes and developments within your organisation which could affect the industry as a whole.
- Briefing a newly-appointed editor or specialist writer on your company and its activities and the service you have to offer.
- A 'thank you' for successful co-operation throughout the year, usually coupled with a briefing on the coming year.
- An introduction for yourself to editor or specialist writers in an area of the media which is new to you.
- A general briefing for editors or journalists with whom you are not often in contact, usually coupled with ideas for specific features.
- To introduce new senior members of your organisation to key journalists.

The question of where to entertain is a function both of your budget and the inclination of your guest. It might be a pleasant gesture to ask your guest where he or she would like to go. On the other hand if you have reasonable in-house facilities this might be a better venue as it will be free from distraction.

It is sometimes even more valuable to entertain a group of journalists together. This can serve both as a briefing meeting and as a discussion group. It is a good idea, for example, to gather together representatives of your immediate trade or industrial publications, together with specialist writers from the national media, at a briefing lunch on the forthcoming year. Such an event enables the senior personnel within your company to meet the leading journalists in the field and to tell them first hand of the company's plans for the coming year. The journalists can ask their questions direct and can also air any grievances or problems in an informal atmosphere.

It is important that the senior management is briefed to be as open as possible at such meetings, otherwise the value of them tends to be diminished. The representatives of the media should see the meeting as a constructive activity and not just a propaganda exercise.

Another example of extremely useful group entertaining is illustrated by a luncheon organised by an organisation which was moving into sports sponsorship for the first time. Leading journalists covering the particular sport were invited to attend the lunch and to give their views on how the sponsorship could best benefit the sport and on how they would like to be kept in the picture. The lunch also served the purpose of introducing the company's executives to this particular section of the media, and a good deal was learnt about how to get the most out of the sponsorship.

Some companies operating in the consumer field have also seen the value of group luncheons in generating special features around products which are not very exciting and which do not really merit a series of individual lunches. Journalists must be told that this is a speculative lunch with only a small information content and that the general intent is to discuss the subject in broad terms with the injection of a few ideas from the PROs. The discussion around the table often generates even better feature ideas which can be taken up by one of the journalists present. The trick is to ensure that there are no magazines represented which compete directly with each other. A luncheon to talk about nail care and nail care products might take in one representative of each of the following types of publication: general women's interest magazines, teenage publications, DIY magazines, holiday magazines, regional newspaper, London office women's editors, retirement publications and secretarial magazines. There is very little clash of interests here and it will be quite obvious which magazine will be interested in which idea.

Checklist for informal entertaining

1 Entertain only if you have a good reason for doing so and only if you have something of value to impart to the guest.

2 Decide whether it will serve your purpose better to entertain individually or in a group.

3 Make sure that personnel who are to be present from sections other than the PR department are fully briefed on their role and on what can and cannot be said.

4 Have a variety of ideas ready to throw into the conversation and listen carefully to the resulting discussion. Make a note of all requests made for further information and of any interest expressed in ideas for features.

Follow-up

Whatever the means of communication has been it is important to follow up properly. If a specific idea has been discussed over the phone confirm the details in writing. If an outline idea has been discussed over the lunch table ring up to carry it further, and if you have floated an idea by post and have heard nothing phone up to see if it has fallen on stony ground. And when an idea has been fully agreed make sure that you deliver on time. But whatever you do, do not send out a general mailing and then ring up and ask whether the recipient is going to use it or not. If they are, your phone call will merely be a slight irritant, but if there is no appropriate slot at that particular time your call could cause enough irritation to prevent the material ever seeing the light of day.

Cuttings

It is useful to have a record of the coverage which has been achieved by the ongoing media relations programme, and a collection of cuttings is one way of doing this.

A number of companies who specialise in press cuttings can be found listed in the current *Hollis Press and Public Relations Annual*. They are usually quite good at cutting daily national papers and the leading magazines, but they tend to be variable in their coverage of specialist magazines and of regional media. It usually makes sense to provide the chosen agency with a media list for large mailings as well as a complete list of specialised magazines in your field. It is also well worth considering the use of two agencies. You could find that the overlap is as little as 50 per cent.

Talk in detail about your requirements to the various companies before making your decision. Once a company is appointed, make sure that they are kept up to date and are encouraged to remain alert to your requirements. It is not a bad idea to change one agency every few years.

Some managements set great store by cuttings but a tally of the column inches or volume of press cuttings does not really tell you all that much. What is much more important is an analysis of the coverage achieved. Is it in the most influential publications for your market or is it in small publications with a limited circulation?

Any report on coverage should also include radio and TV, and here tapes and transcripts are as useful as a time assessment in showing the quality of the coverage. There are companies which specialise in recording this kind of material, but they tend to be rather expensive. If you are organising a series of local radio interviews, a simple request to each station for a recording of the broadcast will usually result in the interviewee being handed the recording at the end of the interview, but you must provide the tape.

It is also worth mentioning here that the PRO's job should be a two-way one. So far we have been talking about the flow of information from the company, but it can be equally important for management to receive information on how the world is thinking about the company and its activities, about rival companies and about the industry in which it operates. Thus a press monitoring service becomes even more important. If your organisation is involved in foreign markets then reaction in these countries would also be important.

Summary of Chapter 6

1   Do not underestimate the value of a helpful, efficient and creative information service.
2   Make sure that everyone who is likely to answer media enquiries is fully briefed on the company and its activities, products and service and has a list of those people who are competent to speak to the media on specialist areas.
3   Find out the background of any query with a view to providing in-depth information.
4   Check on the telephone manners of everyone who is likely to answer media enquiries by ringing in yourself; ensure that the attitude of everyone is helpful and friendly.
5   Fulfil press requests for information, photographs and samples immediately. Send material by mini-cab if necessary and always phone back within 24 hours if there is any delay at all in providing the material.
6   Make a list of material which could generate ongoing coverage over a three-or six-month period and work out a plan for offering both general releases and specific feature material.

7 Keep in constant contact with key media.

8 Send only to non-competing regional publications and think up creative and original ideas for national and leading specialist media.

9 Make the decision to entertain a rational one and ensure that you have something useful to impart or to discuss.

10 Decide whether individual or group entertaining will be more appropriate to a particular objective.

11 Make sure that when ideas for features are to be discussed in a group setting there are no competitive media present.

12 Follow up specific ideas but do not pester the media after general mailings.

13 Institute a sensible system for checking on TV, radio and press coverage.

14 Assess results in terms of quality as well as quantity.

7 Techniques for television and radio

One of the results of an active media relations service is likely to be requests for spokesmen for radio and television programmes, and special events and launches could lead to live coverage or even to a programme being made on the subject. However, requests from the media can also come to the PR department as a result of disasters, strikes and general controversy.

Deciding whether or not to appear

The very first step is to try and ascertain exactly why the media have approached you. Never accept any invitation, however flattering it may appear, without first checking it. Here are a few questions to ask.

- Why are they making the programme? Do they have any particular angle in mind?
- Why have they approached your organisation rather than a competitor?

- What was the source of their initial information if any? Ask for a copy of the original information so that any spokesman you provide will not have it sprung upon him.
- Is the programme to be live or recorded?
- Are they planning to use any film or other material or props you and your spokesman should know about?
- Can they give you an idea of the questions which will be asked?

The answers to some or all of these questions will give you a much clearer idea of what the request is all about. Of course, there will be many occasions when the request is a direct result of your own work and you will not need to be quite so suspicious. A request for the appearance of an author of a sponsored book or for an expert on holidays in the Far East is unlikely to cause any problems, but it is still sensible to obtain full details of the programme concerned.

The next step is to decide whether or not to go ahead. Many organisations seemed to have an in-built reluctance to defend their actions or even to provide a constructive and forceful image. This is sometimes due to a generally secretive approach but it is probably more often because of a fear of being made to appear inadequate at the hands of an experienced interviewer. However, this is more surely an argument for adequate preparation than for a refusal to appear.

The PRO's role here is one of guidance. The benefits and disadvantages of putting up a spokesman or providing filming facilities should be weighed with care and the validity of the company or client's position in relation to the topic must be discussed with senior management. You will need to warn management of the potentially adverse effects of refusing to appear or to comment and this will need to be set against the fact that having a valid argument does not always guarantee a sympathetic audience.

Sometimes too much can be expected of an opportunity to put forward the company's point of view. On the other hand, failure to do so may lose the opportunity altogether. There is little right of reply on radio and television and even where it exists it is not particularly likely to be heard by the audience of the original programme. However, in most circumstances the right decision will be to go ahead and at this point the PRO must, as honestly as possible, judge the merits of his company's case and, if necessary, suggest ways in which the company might modify its stance on an issue so as to reduce its vulnerability.

Training for TV and radio

Speaking on TV and radio is a technique in itself. It makes practical sense to train suitable spokesmen. There is no point in special efforts to arrange TV and radio coverage if you do not have anyone qualified to appear. Occasionally the public relations executive of an organisation is also that organisation's spokesman but, except for promotional and marketing campaigns where the PRO is indeed the expert in the area, the provision of an obvious intermediary can lead to the viewer seeing him as a buffer for those who might more usefully have appeared.

It is far better to offer the relevant expert in the field. The line manager will know much more about his production process and the home economist will have the food facts at her fingertips. Provided that they have been well trained the specialists are far less likely to be caught out by a clever interviewer. They will also come over much more convincingly to the viewer or radio audience.

Obviously the actual people chosen for training will depend upon the needs of your particular organisation and its PR programme. However, it is always worth considering either the chairman or managing director for training and possibly one or two other members of the board. Top line personnel carry much more authority when really critical matters are at stake. At other times the man in charge of the relevant section or the local man might be a better choice.

If your organisation is a 'high tech' company and works in areas such as microbiology or electronics it will be useful to have a trained scientist who can translate what the company is doing into terms which most people can understand. If, on the other hand, it is concerned with food, with telephone sales or with insurance, the people to train might be home economists, one of the telephone sales force or the area sales manager. Some companies have successfully trained teams of staff based across the country who are able to speak for the company on everything but board level decisions.

Of course, TV and radio training can be expensive both in the cost and the time involved in the training itself and in time lost from work making broadcasts, but it can also pay off extremely well. A national telephone directory gained extremely good coverage on local radio by training two of their telephone sales girls to talk about their work, and some government departments also achieve a high degree of positive coverage by training staff to take part in advice and phone-in programmes.

There are a number of companies which specialise in this type of training. Look for names in the Yellow Pages of the *Hollis Annual*. Some of these companies also specialise in making tapes for syndication to local radio and with a strong topical theme this kind of approach can achieve a good deal of coverage without taking up too much of an executive's time. Alternatively outside experts or personalities whose views coincide with those of the company may be used. Make sure that there is adequate follow-up included in the deal so that you will know how and where the tape was used and can assess its value for future PR programmes.

Working with TV producers and crews

Once the decision has been made to accept an invitation from the media you will need to know what form the programme is to take. If there is to be live filming of an event as an outside broadcast the technicians will soon enough explain the facilities which they will need for lighting, position of cameras and so on. You will certainly need to make arrangements for the siting of the outside broadcast van and the laying of cables. If the crew are likely to be on site for some time a thought about refreshments will also be very welcome. Careful timing will also be required to ensure that the item is actually happening at the time it fits into the programme.

Filmed events are much easier to handle, but even so there will still be quite a large team from the TV company. Make sure that they have everything they need and that they have been thoroughly briefed, but do leave them alone to do their job. A hovering PRO will only be in the way.

If you are involved in sponsored events a knowledge of camera sites and angles will be particularly important. First of all there are usually banner sites to choose, and there is no point in having these running counter to the tracking of the camera. There are also small promotional touches which a resourceful PRO can introduce, such as girls in suitable uniforms, marshals' anoraks and badges. Take care, though, not to overdo it. One national company succeeded so well in getting its slogan onto the race course during a sponsored meeting that the TV company refused to film again unless some of the items were removed.

If there are to be company spokesmen involved in the filming, it is your job to make sure that they are there when they are wanted and that they have been briefed on what to say. If there is any chance of 'doorstepping' or having a microphone pushed under their noses as they are leaving a meeting make sure that they know this might happen. A few carefully prepared words worked out between the conference room and the door will do the job and there is no need to say any more. A polite refusal to comment further is far better than a panic reply.

Studio programmes

Studio programmes present quite different problems, so before briefing the person who has been chosen to represent your organisation recheck the background as outlined on page 109. To these questions the following may also need to be added.
- What are the names of the programme producer and director?
- What is the time of the recording or broadcast?
- Can your spokesman have a preview of other relevant material to be shown on the programme?
- Will your company be able to show its own film, pictures, models or sample products?
- Will there be others appearing in the programme and if so who?
- Will there be a studio audience and will questions be allowed from the floor?

Some programmes are made up of a straight interview, but your spokesman may not actually be in the same studio as the interviewer. In this instance it is very important for him to look at the monitor while talking and try to pretend that the interviewer is in the room with him.

On other occasions your spokesman may be taking part in a panel discussion. In this instance don't choose someone who is too polite and retiring–they may have to talk over the opposition to get their point across!

Preparation

There is no such thing as over-preparation. The more rehearsed the better the spokesman or interviewee will be. Whatever you do, never let anyone from your company appear on TV or radio without preparation. There is nothing worse than improvisation. Useful books in this area are *Be Your Own PR Man* by Michael Bond, published by Kogan Page, and *You're on Next! How to survive on TV and radio* by the same author and publisher.

The briefing obtained from the producer is the best starting point, but remember that for perfectly legitimate reasons this might be changed. Ask yourself what needs to be said and relay the gist of this to your spokesman, who can then put it into his or her own words. It is a good idea actually to write out in simple words the points that need to be made. There should never be more than two or three essential points, for you will never get enough time to make any more. Subdivide each point into simple statements and then ask yourself whether the point will immediately be grasped by someone who knows nothing about the subject.

Encourage your spokesman to use everyday language and, if there are large figures to put across, use analogies which will mean something to the listener. These points, figures, and analogies must be fixed in the memory so that they can be brought out at the appropriate moment. It is also sensible to anticipate all the questions likely to be asked, particularly the potentially embarrassing ones. Answers to these will also need to be worked out and if possible these answers should be framed in such a way that the points you want to make can be slid in as well. Don't spend too much of the answer defending your organisation; simply make a quick answer and move on to more positive points.

Writing out notes helps to fix items in the memory, but it is not a good idea to use notes in a TV interview, as one of the effects of television is to diminish the speaker's authority if he has to refer to notes continually. On the other hand, notes can be extremely useful for radio, particularly for long phone-ins where there may be quite a few questions which require detailed instructions in the answer. Type such notes on one side of the paper and limit them to three or four sheets which can be laid out in front of you and not moved during the programme.

Your spokesman will also need some advice on dress for television. Flamboyant clothes are a mistake unless they are a genuine part of the interviewee's personality.

Wear clothes which are appropriate to the interview; conventionally this might be a business suit or smart sportswear. If the interview is to be on-site then usual working clothes will be more appropriate. Two-piece clothing is quite useful for women as the microphone and battery can be fixed and concealed in it more easily than a dress.

At the studio

Here are some guidelines for in-studio behaviour and some tips on handling potentially difficult interviews. Discuss the various points with your spokesman.

Before the programme:

Most producers go to considerable lengths to help calm newcomers down. You can help by arriving either on time or with a little time to spare.

Ask to meet the interviewer and, if this request is granted, ask him what he is going to ask you. However, do not make the mistake of answering him there and then. Reserve your answer for the cameras, or you may inadvertently give him more fuel for his theme. In fact don't talk about your subject at all. Chat and be friendly but take care not to say anything to anybody that you might regret. Nothing is off the record here.

Very often drinks are dispensed in the TV hospitality rooms. *Never* have a drink before going on. Afterwards is the time to relax, not before   Allow the studio make-up girl to make you up. The studio lighting can make you look grim if you do not. This goes for women as much as for men; street make-up is not suitable.

Before the programme starts you will be invited to say a few words for the sound balance. Don't just count; tell them how you got to the studio or what you had for breakfast. This gives the technicians a better idea of your voice and relaxes you.

During the programme:

Do not sit back too comfortably in your chair: this can look very complacent. Sit on the edge of your chair. This makes you look alert, as indeed you will have to be in order not to fall off! Forget the cameras and everyone else in the studio and talk to and look at the interviewer or the members of the panel. This really is not as difficult as it sounds as the strong lights black out the background and the cameras are surprisingly easy to ignore. A sound studio is actually likely to be much more distracting as you will usually be able to see the engineers and technicians working away in the control room and researchers or producers may be passing notes to the presenter. Try to be as sincere and enthusiastic as possible and be conversational – you are not addressing a public meeting.

Do not hesitate before answering a question. This makes even the most honest of answers seem indecisive and uncertain. Avoid saying 'I think' as this, too, is not positive enough. The viewers will think that you do not know the answer.

Never say 'No comment'. If you cannot comment say why not. The matter may be *sub judice* or there may be other people to consult.

When you have answered a question or made a point, be quiet. Don't fall for the 'pregnant pause' gambit. The interviewer wants you to go burbling on–you may say something indiscreet. However, the interview is his responsibility and he cannot allow a silence to last for too long.

At the end of your programme:

Stay in your chair until you are told it is all right to get up – the camera may still be on you. For the same reason you should not make any comment other than innocuous ones until the microphone has been removed.

Radio interviews

Much of what has been said with reference to TV also applies to radio. On the whole, radio stations are friendlier places than TV stations and have a good deal of time to fill with non-controversial general interest material.

If at all possible it is best for the interviewee to go to the studio. However, as a last resort the telephone can be used. The trouble here is that all enthusiasm tends to be lost and the interview can sound very flat. Remove all distractions in the vicinity of the phone and try to speak with firmness and decision. Do not try to listen to the radio at the same time as this can cause 'feedback' down the phone.

Sometimes studio interviews are conducted over the air with an interviewer in London or Glasgow and the interviewee in Birmingham or Manchester. Headphones will have to be worn for this type of interview. They will also need to be worn for phone-in programmes. Incidently when doing phone-ins it's a good idea to write down each person's name as they call in so that you can address them by name. Make sure too that you have the answers to questions which may require actual information–this can be taken in note form.

The microphones in a radio studio always tend to be large and rather obtrusive. The trick is to try and look beyond them to the interviewer and talk as though the two of you are having a personal conversation. Try to interest him or her in what you have to say and the chances are that you will also interest the audience. Try to keep still and avoid knocking the table or microphone or shuffling your chair or papers.

It is quite a good idea to take along samples to a radio interview. It is much easier to talk about something or explain if you have it in front of you and even though the listener cannot actually see it you will be able to paint a mental picture for him. The representative of one small electrical cooking appliance manufacturer achieved excellant coverage by offering to cook breakfast actually in the studio for local DJs, and interviews with cookery authors are often backed up with sample dishes to taste in the studio.

Of course, quite a number of radio interviews take place outside the studio and, unless a particular background buzz is wanted to give atmosphere to the tape, a quiet place to record will be needed. Here again the technique is to try to ignore the microphone and talk directly to the interviewer. Remember that most people tend to drop their voices at the end of a sentence. This should be avoided on radio, but otherwise speak as you normally speak–do not try for a 'BBC' or any other accent. National regional accents sound very attractive on radio.

Liaison with other departments

To get the most out of TV and radio appearances it is sensible to inform other departments in your organisation who can capitalise on it that the piece will be appearing. If there is some doubt that the item will go out, send the information out directly after the broadcast. The sales department, for example, or the export department if the broadcast is to go out on the world service or in any particular language, might be able to use the information to back up sales activity and to show that promotional support is being given to the company's product or services.

Internal relations will also be furthered if those who have featured on filmed material are told when they might expect to see themselves, and the company personnel as a whole will be interested in watching a programme featuring their company.

Summary of Chapter 7

1   Find out the reasons for any request for spokesmen or filming facilities and try to ascertain what angle is to be taken.

2   The decision to appear should be taken only after a careful look at the benefits and disadvantages of doing so.

3   Make sure that the organisation has a small number of executives trained to speak on subjects which are likely to come up and that there is at least one board member who can represent the company in times of serious criticism or comment.

4   Once the decision has been taken to go ahead, be as co-operative as possible. Smooth the way for outside broadcasts and film units and check on props and samples needed for studio work.

5   Make a complete check of the proposed programme and how it is to be put together so that you can thoroughly brief your spokesman or interviewee.

6   Make sure that the chosen spokesman has thoroughly prepared for the interview and knows both the answers to difficult questions and the positive points he wants to get across.

7   Brief your spokesman carefully on what to expect at the studios and run through some general do's and don'ts for the interview itself.

8   Inform interested parties within your organisation who may be able to capitalise on the broadcast that the item will appear or has appeared.

8 Bought editorials, competitions and special offers

Most publications are on the lookout for ways of increasing their circulation and some are also looking for extra revenue. This means that both the editors and the promotion department of a particular publication may be interested in 'advertorials', associated booklets, competitions and special offers. The fact that a particular publication does not offer these types of promotion on a regular basis does not mean that it will not be interested in discussing a bright idea. And though it is usually consumer publications that are involved there have been some notable exceptions among even the more staid members of the trade press.

These promotional tools can be extremely useful to the discerning PRO, particularly for products and services which have passed their first peak of interest. The first advantage to the participating company of all of these types of activity is that they are not seen by the reader as advertising but as part of the editorial content of the magazine and therefore as having the endorsement of the editorial staff. This is true even though the approach may vary from a fairly soft sell in the 'advertorial' to quite a strong sales pitch in the special offer.

The second advantage is that such promotions enable the name of your organisation or its brands to be included in the copy, which can be very important in publications which would not normally use such names. The choice between the different types of bought space outlined below will depend partly on the product or service in question and partly on the available budget. It will also depend upon which type of promotion the editor is prepared to tolerate in his or her pages, for the choice of medium is as important here as many other parts of the media programme. The best advertorial in the world will be of no value at all if it is aimed at the wrong audience.

Advertorials

A relatively new phenomenon is the paid-for editorial, whose rather ugly jargon name is 'advertorial'. This usually takes the form of an eight-page booklet bound into the magazine and looking to all intents and purposes like any other part of the publication. The difference is that the copy has been supplied by a PRO and the photography and space have been paid for by that PRO's company or organisation. In a sense the advertorial is an extension of the illustrated feature article discussed in Chapters 4 and 6. It is normally found in magazines rather than in newspapers, where the far less subtle advertising feature has been well established for years.

Advertorials are a godsend to PROs who have the unenviable task of promoting everyday products such as soup, shampoo, paint, weedkiller or garden tools. The products are good enough to need little in the way of re-vamping and apart from the odd addition to the range or a change of packaging little of any interest happens to the product. But the PRO is charged with keeping it in the public eye. Even fashion products such as nail polish or lipstick, which do have regular changes of colour, can benefit greatly.

The contents

In theory an advertorial could be put together on almost any subject appropriate to the magazine and to the sponsor. In practice it has mainly been used in the fields of food, cooking and beauty. But there is no reason why an enterprising PRO might not put together any package which would be of interest to the general consumer. A gardening magazine might be interested in advertorials on growing certain types of plant on different soils or on dealing with pests. Obvious sponsors might be seed merchants or weedkiller manufacturers.

Similarly, holiday route guides or DIY maintenance might be of interest to motoring magazines, with car or accessory manufacturers as sponsors. Home decorating and colour scheming advertorials might be offered by paint and wallpaper companies; indeed the opportunities are many and varied.

The mechanics

The mechanics of the advertorial vary. Sometimes the copy and photographs are provided by the sponsor as a package. However, this can have problems, as the editorial staff of the magazine will want to have some input. Similarly a piece written by the magazine staff could have problems for the sponsor. However, the editorial staff are often too busy to do the work and an outside expert is called in to write the piece in consultation with both sides. If this expert knows the product or has already worked with it, so much the better.

Where photography is involved–and it usually is–it is even more important to get the style right. After all, the advertorial is intended to look as much like the other editorial pages as possible. Arrange a briefing meeting with representatives of the magazine and the sponsor, the author and the photographer to make sure that everyone knows exactly what is required.

The cost of any advertorial will depend upon the publication and the size of its circulation. If the cost is higher than your budget will stand it is possible to collaborate with one, two or even three other manufacturers to put together a bumper bundle. One national women's magazine recently carried an advertorial with no fewer than ten participating, but of course non-competing, manufacturers. However, you might well think that some of the impact is lost in such an exercise.

Booklets

Associated booklets distributed with a magazine are another form of bought space, though they are a little less subtle in approach in that they are not bound into the publication and may have a different format. However, the editorial endorsement may still be fairly strong in that the booklet may carry the name of the magazine in its own title such as the 'Modern Woman's Guide to House Buying'. It may or may not go on to say 'produced in conjunction with brand X or company Y'.

The content of such a booklet is very similar to that of an advertorial. There is a relatively soft sell of the company's products or services and the copy is as useful as possible. The idea is to create goodwill by producing a really helpful guide or a series of ideas which will be of use to customers and potential customers. However, the shape and length of the booklet may be planned with effective presentation in mind. It will not be as limited by the size and shape of the magazine as the advertorial.

Distribution in conjunction with a particular publication can be expensive both in the distribution fee and in the cost of producing so many copies. It might therefore be worth considering the alternative of independent production and printing, relying on editorial mention for distribution. Booklets can be very popular indeed and some booklets have been taken up in very large quantities.

Checklist for advertorials and booklets

1 Choose a subject which will be of interest to the readers of the magazine concerned and which will illustrate the best use of your organisation's range of products.

2 The content must, first of all, be useful to the reader. Any attempt to introduce the sponsor's range of products must be low key. This is not an advertisement in the usual sense.

3 Consider who is best qualified to write the copy. An independent or outside expert may be the answer.

4 Make sure that the photography or drawn illustrations are in keeping with the editorial image of the magazine.

5 Look at the costs involved and if these seem too high for your budget, consider joining with non-competing manufacturers.

6 Before committing yourself compare the various costs, advantages and disadvantages of advertorials against booklets.

Special offers

Special offers fall into two main categories: those which are really free giveaways or are very cheap indeed and those which offer relatively expensive items at a discount.

Free offers

Free giveaways are almost always associated with new products and form part of the sampling operation which is often necessary for the public to acquire a taste for them. They may be physically attached to the front cover of the publication, slipped between the pages or offered on the editorial pages.

Items which are physically attached to the front cover gain in that they could not really be more prominently displayed and are bound to reach all the purchasers of the magazine. But they do need to be small enough to fit on the cover without taking up much space, and light enough not to tear the paper. Packaging can also cause a headache.

Slipping between the pages of a magazine may work for a sachet of shampoo or for a soup mix, but the product can very easily slip out again and the end purchaser may not receive the sample.

Offers made on the editorial pages need to be particularly attractive or the readers will not take the trouble to send off their stamped addressed envelope. With all these promotions you must be prepared to give away quite large numbers of the product. The magazine may have a circulation of half a million or more. Even with editorial offers the magazine will want to be sure that stocks will not give out too soon, or they will have a great many disappointed readers.

Discount offers

Special offers involving a discount, on the other hand, can both promote the product and bring in some revenue. However, magazines will drive a hard bargain and if you are to enjoy the advantages of full page coverage you will have to offer a very good discount, guarantee stocks and pay a handling fee.

A problem arises with sample offers if you are not geared up for individual direct mail dispatch. Of course, you can hand the whole thing over to a direct mail house but there may still be additional and expensive packaging to design and pay for.

For some companies special offers are more difficult because their product may only be used by professionals, such as hairdressers, or it may be perishable and not suitable for selling through the post. Money-off vouchers are one answer, but they are not very popular with magazines and may not be well received by suppliers either. If you do try to use them you must be very sure that they will be honoured or you will be generating bad rather than goodwill.

Checklist for special offers

1   Does the cost of the product in question point to a free offer or a discount?

2   Is the product or sample small enough to slip between the pages of the magazine or can it easily be attached to the front cover?

3   Are you prepared to fulfil quite large demands for the sample or offer?

4   How is the discounted product to be dispatched and how is it to be protected en route? What is the cost of this?

5   If vouchers are under consideration will retailers be happy with the redemption system?

Editorial competition

A competition is another device for promoting your product or services by name in terms of both write-up and pictures. Most types of publication and indeed some radio stations will consider competitions. They are fun for their readers or audience and offer a chance to win something for nothing or at least for a very slight effort.

Of course, the prizes are crucial. Ideally they should be associated with your product or services. They are also the means of 'buying' your way into the publication. Publications which run editorial competitions on a regular basis usually have a set price level, which may vary from as little as £50 or £100 value for a small provincial weekly to around £20,000-£25,000 for a national women's magazine. There may also be a handling fee.

The prize structure

Bearing in mind that it is essential to include your own product somewhere in the prize structure, consider the size of the top prize *vis-à-vis* the second tier of prizes, whether there should be more than two tiers of prizes or whether there should be, say, 50 or 100 prizes of equal weight. Discuss these questions with the magazine's promotions department. They have the experience of many hundreds of competitions to call upon.

An electrical equipment manufacturer, for example, might decide to go for a fully-fitted kitchen including all their own appliances as the top prize, with a small number of runners-up receiving a toaster or sandwich maker. Alternatively the choice might be ten top prizes of the latest cooker with a larger number of small runner-up prizes or with two tiers of second- or third-level prizes.

Where the sponsor's product is low in value there may be 100 or 500 second- or third-tier prizes, the top prizes being taken from other organisations in the form of holidays, cars or even cash. The latter is popular with the public but not with the sponsor, there being little chance of a discount!

The format

After the prize structure has been established the next most important decisions will concern the competition format. This must be designed to attract entrants, but you will also want it to focus attention on your organisation and its products. To some extent the format will depend upon the chosen publication and the likely number of entrants. If you are expecting thousands of entries the format will need to be such that it is easy to eliminate incorrect entries. A competition which requires every entry to be judged on its creative content, for example, would be impossible here.

Ideas for large-scale competitions are many and varied. They could involve matching a variety of situations or uses to a list of products or a list of items using those products; they could involve putting the benefits of the product in order of merit or they could take the form of a question and answer quiz with specified answers from which to choose.

All of these ideas can be prejudged for the correct answers, which can then be very quickly matched against each entry. They also have the advantage of having a great many permutations and combinations and this will cut the number of correct entries to a minimum, thus making final judging much easier.

In addition to the above format there must also be a tie-breaker. This gives the final level of judging between all the correct entries. This tie-breaker lends itself even more than the general format of the competition to focusing attention on the product in hand. 'I think brand X is the best because . . . ' is the theme of most tie-breakers.

This type of format can also be used where a smaller number of entrants is expected, but these competitions do offer an opportunity for getting some useful creative ideas from the public. Designs for cake decorations, recipes using a particular product, advertising slogans and the like could be the basis of the competition. Do not forget, however, to include a clause in the rules stating that the sponsor will take the copyright of all entries.

This type of competition may take much longer to judge as the judges will have to look at all the entries. Similar ideas, some of which will come up rather frequently, can be removed by a preliminary screening, but there will still be a great deal to get through, so warn the judges in advance.

Another disadvantage of this type of competition is that it may look just a little too difficult and thus put off some of the would-be entrants. This might not matter too much if they have read all the competition copy first, but it is a point to watch. Local regional newspaper competitions should be particularly straightforward and simple to enter or the entry figures will be disappointing.

Judges and rules

The choice of judges is fairly important and getting one or two well-known personalities on the panel could be a booster for the competition. In any event, you will need to have at least one independent judge who is unconnected with either the company or the publication.

The formulation of the rules is another easily overlooked, but very important, area. You do not necessarily need to take up space by publishing them with the competition but they must be readily available on request. It is probably worth taking advice from a specialist competitions house when organising your first big competition. However, here are a few points to include.

1   Closing date for entries and address to which entries should be sent.
2   Prohibition of entry to anyone working for the companies involved in the competition, including the sponsers, publishing house and competition handlers, advertising or public relations consultants.
3   Statement that the judges' decision is final and that no correspondence will be entered into.
4   Statement on copyright in the designs, ideas or slogans.
5   Statement on elimination of incomplete, unreadable or changed entries.
6   Statement that proof of posting will not be taken as proof of receipt of an entry.
7   Statement that there is no cash alternative.

Dispatch of prizes

The next stage in the planning should concern the dispatch of prizes to the winners. This is usually fairly easy to arrange if the prize is a holiday or a large piece of equipment and if the prize structure is fairly small. However, there may be quite large quantities of product to send out and special packaging may be needed. So liaise in good time with either your own dispatch department or an outside mail order company. This usually all works well with a large one-off competition, but if you have organised a series of regional newspaper competitions, for example, you will need to have a foolproof system to ensure that winners receive their prizes shortly after winning and you do not have irate editors ringing up saying that their readers are growing angry at the lack of delivery.

Follow-up

For the enterprising PRO the job does not end with the announcement of the winners. With a national competition there will be some very valuable regional coverage to organise. The media in the winner's area may be interested in an interview and the newspapers will almost certainly take pictures of the presentation ceremony. Similarly, if runners-up win substantial prizes, arrange where possible for the handover to be on the premises of a local supplier. This will not only achieve your regional publicity; it will help to create goodwill within the trade and may even give you some material for the appropriate trade press.

Checklist for editorial competitions
1   What are you hoping to achieve by the competition? The answer to this question could affect the rest of the checklist.

Checklist: continued

2 What kind of prize structure is most appropriate to your product range and does this fit in with the experience of the publication?

3 Plan the competition format to maximise the publicity value of the competition bearing in mind ease of entry and ease of judging.

4 Draw up the rules with the legal requirements in mind and make sure that everything is covered.

5 Organise the packing and dispatch of prizes.

6 Plan a follow-up programme of media activity to maximise the benefits of the competition.

9 Receptions and conferences

From time to time you need to inform more than a handful of journalists about significant events or changes within your organisation and you will be tempted to say 'let's have a press conference'. Certainly senior management will be keen to have one – indeed it is often very difficult to persuade the senior executive that he is not quite the captain of industry that he imagines himself to be and that the media will not necessarily hang upon his every word.

All kinds of events will make a good story, but a full-scale press conference is not necessarily the most effective way of broadcasting it. Press conferences can cost a considerable amount of money, which will be money ill-spent if the media feel that their time has been wasted.

Preliminary planning

Is the conference really necessary?

Every time the idea of a press conference is mooted, scrutinise it closely. You should be certain that the information cannot be usefully imparted in any other way. Ask the following questions and if there are no affirmative answers the chances are that a telex message, a mailing backed up by personal contact or some other means of communication will be more efficient.

1   Is the news such that speed of communication is of the essence?
2   Is there some important 'hard' news to impart, such as the discovery of a new and revolutionary drug, an announcement of a project which will create new employment opportunities or a big export contract?
3   Is there a complicated scientific or technical angle to the story which requires the presence of experts to explain or demonstrate it?
4   Does the story concern products to which people do not generally have access and which can be put on show?
5   Is the product so new and different that it must be seen or sampled in person to understand what it is all about?
6   Is there a fashion element to the product which needs to be seen?

All too often the answer to each of these questions is 'No, not really. But . . . ' The 'but' is usually that the marketing department, (or, if you are working in a consultancy, the client) wants a press conference and of course the PRO likes to be seen to be doing something. Nor are the reasons always spurious. A press conference for 'soft' news such as product launches and the like is often seen as an opportunity to meet journalists in influential media and to entertain–following the traditional notion that the press will never turn down an invitation to drink. While this may be true in individual cases, most journalists are too busy to indulge in massive lunchtime drinking, and the last thing they want to do is to waste time going to a press conference to hear about something which is exactly like everything else on the market or which they could have sampled by post.

Meeting journalists is far better organised informally as outlined in Chapter 6. Everyone knows that the object of the exercise is an informal chat or a reminder of the potential of existing products and each journalist can decide whether or not the time will be well spent. Sadly it is often impossible to tell from the invitation to a product launch whether it will be worth attending. Too many invitations to time-wasting events alienate the media.

Timing

When a press conference is decided upon, timing will be very important. An important story will need to be released as soon as possible after all the facts are known to the organisation, or there will be a danger of the story breaking in an uncontrolled way. Some events will need immediate reaction, while others can be held for a short period while detailed arrangements are made.

Sometimes the timing is governed by factors external to the PR department, such as the publication date of financial results or market survey reports, the start of an advertising campaign for a new product or the date set for the signing of a contract. Product availability can be another stumbling block for the PRO organising a big product launch. You must be sure that the product will be available to display or demonstrate and possibly to sample at the press conference. Ideally it should also be about to appear in the shops so that any immediate coverage in daily media is not lost. Another problem can arise when the product is on sale only in one part of the country or if it has not yet been fully sold into the trade.

National media will want to be sure that all their readers can obtain the product.

However, where the timing is flexible from the company point of view the following considerationswill also need to be taken into account.

- Availability of key personnel from within the company
- Availability of celebrities, models and the like
- Availability of a suitable venue
- The time required to send out invitations and receive replies
- The time required to put together the presentation with display material and visual aids
- The time required to produce press packs
- The press dates of important publications

This last consideration will probably cause the biggest problems. The actual question here is when you want the coverage to occur. If the answer is a specific time such as Christmas, early March or the middle of September there will be a problem with the lead times of the various publications. If the monthly media are as important to you as the weeklies or the dailies the press launch will have to be held up to six months before – Christmas in June parties are commonplace – and the daily media are recontacted much nearer the time.

If, however, there is a chance that the daily media will break the story too soon, it may be worth selecting a small number of the most influential of the monthly publications and letting them have the information in advance. The launch can then be held much nearer to the coverage date that you have in mind.

On other occasions there could be a positive advantage in having the coverage spread over the four- to five-month period that it takes for all types of media to take up and use the material. However, it still makes sense to think up a few exclusive feature ideas for influential monthlies who might otherwise feel that the subject had been fully covered by the dailies and weeklies.

Press dates are also important for quite another

reason. Journalists on weekly publications will not want to be away from the office on press day. So check the actual days of the week on which influential journals are 'put to bed'. The editors of trade journals, particularly, complain about the number of PROs who disregard their press dates and then wonder why they did not turn up at the event.

The time of day can also be important. Breakfast events are quite popular, for guests can attend on their way to the office. However, lunchtime is by far the most normal period. Teatime events can work, but early evening is not a good time–most people want to go home. Finally, it is worth checking to see if there are to be any other functions in the same sphere of interest on the day that you have chosen. In some areas there are special registers of events. If these do not exist in your particular area it may be worth checking the diary of a friendly journalist.

Type and budget

Press conferences can be divided into three main categories. First of all, there is the news conference, which is called when there are immediate announcements to make or there is 'hard' news to impart. The requirements are relatively simple. Refreshments are unlikely to be elaborate and the emphasis is on the speedy transfer of information. Mid-morning is the best time for a news conference, but they can be held at any time of the day. Make sure that there are plenty of phones within easy reach if the story is important.

The second type of press conference is the photocall, an event arranged specifically for photographers. The item or event to be photgraphed may be staged or it may be left *in situ*. Here again the arrangements are uncomplicated, the emphasis being on photographic facilities, and the refreshments will be simple. Like the journalists who attend a news conference, the photographers on a photocall are unlikely to stay very long as they will have other assignments to cover after yours.

The third, and easily the most frequent, type of press

conference is the press reception. This is generally called for 'soft' news items, product launches being by far the most common. The format can vary from something not much more elaborate than the news conference arrangement to a full-scale theatrical presentation.

On the whole news conferences and photocalls do not need very large budgets. However, the press reception can cost very much more and it is important to agree a total budget before planning the details. There is no point in planning an elaborate multi-screen audio-visual show or a song-and-dance spectacular if the budget will only pay for a finger buffet in the advertising agency boardroom.

Money will be the deciding factor in most press conference plans, but its presence or absence should not blind you to the objectives of the event. It is tempting to attempt a thoroughly memorable presentation with a top TV star, but the information may be more appropriately conveyed by your own home economist or DIY expert. Equally, you may like the idea of an elaborate sit-down lunch when the money might be better spent on a room set and painting demonstration.

In fact, in all aspects of planning the criterion must be passing on what you have to say in the most effective manner, in the minimum of time and with the least fuss.

Checklist for the preliminary planning of a press conference

1   Decide whether the press conference is genuinely necessary with reference to the importance and nature of the information to be imparted. Avoid holding press conferences simply to please or impress management.

2   Decide upon the most appropriate timing for the conference bearing in mind constraints within the company, such as product availability, and publication dates.

Checklist: continued

> 3 Leave sufficient time before the conference for all the organisational details to be attended to.
>
> 4 Plan the timing of the coverage in conjunction with the timing of the conference. Fill in gaps by preliminary briefings or personal follow-up.
>
> 5 Decide which category of press conference the information merits and budget accordingly.

Organising the event

The format for news conferences and photocalls

To some extent the format of the press conference will be determined by its purpose. News conferences and photocalls are usually simple affairs, though the latter may sometimes present some operational problems. A cosmetic company launching a brand with a name similar to a particularly fierce type of wild animal decided to have their beauty queen available for photographs with a cub of the animal in question. This event obviously called for special arrangements with regard to safety and insurance, which are not usually necessary!

The news conference layout usually comprises a top table and chairs for the speakers. It is quite a good idea, if time allows, to have printed cards with the spokesmen's names on them. Make sure that they are large enough to be read at the back of the hall. Chairs may also be set out for the media; but if the venue is a factory or office block this may not be possible and it doesn't much matter.

Coffee and a bar will usually be sufficient refreshment, perhaps with a few sandwiches and other finger buffet items if the conference is timed during the lunch hour. If the conference is on your own premises coffee, beer and a couple of spirits with mixers should be sufficient. Add some food if you are situated miles from any kind of catering establishment, but do not be surprised if few stay for it.

Much more important than the refreshments is access to telephones. If the venue is a large hotel there should not be too much difficulty. However, if the story is an important one, you should consider laying on some extra lines. British Telecom will usually be happy to organise temporary lines.

A photocall will need slightly different facilities. Though a journalist can take notes just as well at the back of the room as at the front, photographers must be in the right position and space must be left for them to operate at various angles around the action to be photographed. They will also appreciate it if a little extra lighting is laid on in dark or shadowy surroundings.

In both instances you will need to provide back-up material. The photographers must have full details to enable a caption to be written for the photograph and journalists will want to have the full text of any prepared speeches and perhaps some background facts and figures.

The format for press receptions

Press receptions may be almost as straightforward as a news conference. A very simple but effective idea was used by a leading food company to communicate the results of a major piece of market research. There were three presenters, a professional from a well known TV current affairs programme together with the marketing manager and one of the brand managers. The speakers all sat on the dais in comfortable armchairs with small body microphones. The professional introduced the speakers and asked questions from time to time, and then handled the questions from the floor. The speakers' remarks were reinforced with back-projected figures on a large screen behind them. The result was a relaxed and extremely interesting half-hour.

On the other hand they may be elaborate affairs with a highly professional song-and-dance routine or with a mini-play using stars of current TV sit-coms. If well written the latter can be extremely amusing, and humour is a powerful method of transmitting information. And of course this is what a press reception sets out to achieve. If you have not communicated the main points you have certainly wasted your money and the journalists' time.

The starting point for planning the format of any press reception must be the material to be communicated. Make a list, in very simple words, of the chief points you want to make. The answers to the following questions may provide a few clues as to how best to make them.

1 Would an activity such as tape-cutting or stone-laying ceremony be appropriate?
2 Does the material lend itself to demonstration, tasting or other kinds of sampling?
3 Does the material lend itself to film treatment?
4 Are there any celebrities with special associations or interests in this field (remember this may include senior politicians or businessmen as well as sportsmen and show business personalities)?
5 Is there a fashion element?
6 Does the material lend itself to a humorous treatment?

It is quite easy to lose control at this stage and to produce all kinds of strange ideas. But you must weigh these ideas against two crucial factors: the money available and the time involved. The budget will probably depend upon the importance attached to the subject matter, and even if it has not yet been agreed you will know from previous experience what the level is likely to be.

The time factor refers both to the amount of time you and your staff have available to prepare for the event and rather more important, to the amount of the guests' time the press conference will take up. Journalists are busy people and they have timetables to keep to. Some of them probably covering three or four subject areas and may have a number of events to attend in one day. Others will not want to be away from the office for too long. Forty to forty-five minutes is the absolute maximum unless the subject is particularly difficult to explain.

On-site events

It is often worth exploiting an active element in the news to be imparted. The press release from Tadchester New Town used in Chapter 3 referred to just such an event. The ceremony was a simple tape-cutting enlivened in this instance by the appropriate reference to red tape. The tape on site was indeed bright red and carried the words 'The last piece of red tape in Tadchester'. In other circumstances a grotesquely large pair of scissors might have helped to get the picture printed.

Of course, one of the disadvantages of this type of on-site reception is that, with the exception of the local media, everyone had to come from London. Invitations therefore included the offer of train tickets and arrangements were made to ferry the guests by bus from the railway station to the various points in Tadchester. The programme, which looked like this, was of course sent to all the guests in advance.

TADCHESTER DEVELOPMENT ZONE LAUNCH
DATE
PROGRAMME OF EVENTS

Train leaves Euston Station	7.45 am
Train arrives Tadchester and buses leave for the site of the launch ceremony.	9.30 am
Guest bus also leaves the Civic Centre, Tadchester, to go to the start of the launch ceremony on the first estate.	9.30 am

The Rt. Hon. Mr R. Smith, MP, arrives by helicopter and is welcomed by the Chairman of Tadchester Council.	10.00–10.05 am
Mr Smith officially opens the first English Development Zone by cutting 'the last piece of red tape in Tadchester'.	10.05–10.15 am
Mr Smith is then welcomed by the Chairman of the New Towns Commission, who introduces him to a Director of the AVC Group of Companies.	10.15–10.20 am
Mr Smith presents the ABC group with a lease for land on the first area of the Development Zone.	10.20–10.30 am
Mr Smith and party leave for the second area of the Development Zone.	10.30 am
Mr Smith arrives at Factory 76, Tadchester and performs an opening ceremony for X and Y Foods Ltd.	10.45–10.50 am
Mr Smith holds a PRESS CONFERENCE in Factory 76.	10.50–11.30 am
Mr Smith leaves by helicopter for London.	11.30 am
Coach returns to Tadchester Civic Centre, where a buffet luncheon will be served.	11.30–12.00
Bus leaves for the station for train back to London.	1.30 pm

NB Maps of Tadchester available on request.
For further information contact – the name, address and phone number of the PRO.

The checklist for this event was relatively complicated and co-ordination of the various groups involved was vital. Here's a sample checklist for this type of event.

Checklist for preparing an on-site press reception (using Tadchester example)

1 Travel arrangements from London and provision of maps for those arriving by car.

2 Organising local coaches, including briefing for the drivers.

3 Briefing for welcoming personnel.

4 Close liaison with the minister's private secretary.

5 Helicopter booking, including the provision of map co-ordinates for the various landings.

6 Marking out and cordoning off of the launch ceremony site with provision of tape, scissors and microphones.

7 Briefing of host company, X and Y Foods, in the second area of the Development Zone.

8 Provision of a room for a press conference, coffee and extra telephones.

9 Provision of private interview rooms for TV and radio interviews with the minister.

10 Liaison with the local council on the luncheon arrangements.

11 Provision of press kits with speeches made at the ceremony, background details on the Development Zone concept and on Tadchester New Town.

12 Booking and briefing of own photographer.

Informal press receptions

In times of economic decline the informal press reception is very popular with clients. It need not cost very much, since the only expenses are the venue and the food and drink. Quite often these receptions are held in the boardroom of the company concerned or at the premises of the advertising or PR consultants. They also offer the advantage of enabling journalists to fit the event in with others on the same day. By their very nature these receptions are relaxed affairs and the informal discussion that takes place between the members of your organisation and individual journalists can be very useful. But even these simple events need a lot of attention to detail. Here are some of the points to watch.

Displays

Don't lose sight, in the general informality, of the fact that you have some information to impart. You have not invited the members of the media to waste their time. Very often a display will do part of the work for you. It may illustrate a new product or provide a background to the points which will be made by the speakers. It also provides an interest and a talking point for the guests.

Display boards are invaluable when you are talking about new processes or systems. Product displays, on the other hand, can show the versatility or the fashion uses of the product. A new range of nail polish colours, for example, might be displayed in small cameo settings with matching fashion items such as jewellery, scarves and other accessories. A new type of cheese may be offered for sampling and displayed made up into a variety of different dishes, perhaps with a seasonal or an entertaining theme.

Static displays can even succeed in demonstrating how well a product performs. One of the most effective uses of this type of display was organised for the launch of a new type of wine cooler. Luck was with the organisers, for it was a boiling hot day. Two bottles of wine were on display, each opened and with a thermometer in it, one in the wine cooler and the other on the table. A large chart behind the table recorded the temperature of the wine when it had been taken from the fridge and placed in the display. Every fifteen minutes a white-coated laboratory technician recorded the temperature of the contents of the two bottles on the graph behind. The results were dramatic. The temperature of the wine in the bottle on the table soared while that of the wine in the cooler first went down a little and then remained static for an hour or more.

If you are holding the event in a hotel you may need to check whether anything can be stuck to the walls, if there is sufficient space for a free-standing unit and whether the lighting needs to be supplemented.

Speakers

The choice of speakers is very important even for an informal reception. They should be relaxed and should appear to be talking off the cuff. You, as PRO, however, must make sure that they are not, for that is a sure way to disaster.

Rehearse the speaker or speakers two or three times before the event and make sure that you hear all that they are going to say. It is sensible to try to work closely together on what is to be said. In this way you can ensure that the main points are communicated clearly and concisely. Common faults are:

- Irrelevant diversification
- A condescending approach, particularly when there are mainly women journalists present
- Jokes about the drinking habits of the media or about the fact that the guests are 'only there for the lunch'
- A very hard sell which goes on too long with too many superlatives
- The attempt to avoid difficult questions, which will inevitably be asked at question time or over lunch.

Company personnel

It makes sense from the PR point of view to exploit the presence of a large number of journalists at a reception and to arrange for a fair number of the company's personnel to meet them. However, inviting staff for the sake of it is not a good idea. Salesmen who know and care nothing about the detail of production process or who cannot answer environmental or consumer-oriented questions are a liability, not a help. The PR staff must also be well informed. There is not much point in their being there if they cannot answer simple questions about the prices in the range or its nutritional content. It is also up to you and your staff to meet the representatives of those publications which can be most useful to you.

Audio-visual presentations

There are a number of very good audio-visual techniques which can be used to tell a story when the subject under discussion is too far away to hold the reception *in situ* or when you have a highly technical product to show. Of course, a simple slide presentation may also be used to back up an ordinary presentation by the marketing or brand manager.

Audio-visual presentations vary in complexity from a single slide projector with voice over to a highly sophisticated eight– or ten-projector show. Alternatively, moving film or video tape may be used. Putting together an effective presentation is almost a subject in itself, but here is a short checklist from which to start.

1 What are the chief points to be communicated?
2 How can these best be illustrated?
3 Who is the presentation aimed at?
4 What sort of budget is available?
5 Brief the script writer or production team, giving them any existing visual material.
6 On receipt of the script, organise all the remaining visual material and brief the production company.

Care will be needed to ensure that all the slides are in the correct order and that the equipment is working well–obvious, perhaps, but it is surprising how often the simplest slide presentation goes wrong on the day. Make sure that the people using the equipment know exactly how to work it and are well rehearsed. Arrange to take some back-up equipment and, if the system is very complicated, a technician.

Check the venue too. Is the room large enough or long enough to take the system you are planning? Are there plenty of power points or will you need to take in extra equipment. Are the flexes long enough? Are the plugs of the right type to match the hotel's sockets? The overlooking or checking of small points such as these can make or break an event.

Live demonstrations

Very often the logical way to present a new product is to demonstrate it. Cookery and beauty demonstrations are fairly commonplace, but products like fire extinguishers, decorating material and car maintenance equipment also lend themselves to demonstration, as do a variety of industrial products.

The content

One fire extinguisher manufacturer who had produced a small fire extinguisher suitable for use on all types of small domestic fires decided to stage a demonstration to show how well it could work if the householder was present when the fire started.

The hotel chosen for the reception had a large open car park and agreed to allow the client to stage the fire demonstration there. Two of the British Standard tests for fire extinguishers were set up. One was rather like a large chip pan fire. The other was quite a large construction of criss-cross blocks of wood. The fires were lit and after a set period of time to allow the fires to establish themselves they were extinguished with the product.

The demonstration looked extremely dramatic. On the day one of the journalists present watched the demonstration and then asked if an inexperienced person would be equally successful in extinguishing the fire. On being told that they would, she demanded to try it for herself. A new fire was duly set up and the journalist in question did indeed put out the fire with the extinguisher, thus making the demonstration even better. This event had not been staged, but it might have been a good idea to ask a friendly journalist to make just that demand.

Audience participation in any demonstration always achieves more, but attempts to enforce it can lead to badwill. One PR company insists on journalists cooking part of their own lunch when launching new products for their clients, and this is not always very popular with the guests. However, in fairness to this PRO, the products have been in an area that involves quite different cooking techniques and he obviously believes that just watching a demonstration is not enough.

Another impressive demonstration was staged by the wallpaper manufacturer who had brought out a new type of wall covering which could be put up very quickly indeed. The method used involved pasting the wall rather than the paper, which helped to make decorating easier as well as quicker. A three-sided room set was built at the reception venue and the whole set was covered during the marketing manager's short presentation.

On other occasions fairly simple demonstrations are enlivened by the addition of a few clever ideas. But beware of being too clever. The PRO of a company producing DIY materials decided to brighten up the demonstration of a new product range by featuring their latest sponsored book, published the same day. The idea was to build a large book and to turn the pages as the various subjects came up in the presentation. To complicate matters the author was to carry out the demonstration in a 'Punch and Judy' style booth within the book. The presentation looked stunning, but it caused great problems at the planning stages and turned out to be extremely expensive.

Organisation

The script and the briefing sessions for those taking part are just as important for live demonstrations as they are for an informal or an audio-visual presentation. But even more important are the rehearsals. All too often the speakers and demonstrators have not met together before the day of the presentation and no one has worked out the timing of speech against action. This is particularly important if the demonstrator is to remain silent and work while the presenter is talking.

Here is a plan of action for a live demonstration with two presenters and one demonstrator.

1　Write and agree script and stage directions.
2　Briefing meeting with presenters and demonstrators all together.
3　Checklist of product and equipment required.
4　Visit to venue to check the facilities, electrics etc.
5　Full rehearsal the day before the event preferably at the venue to check timing and equipment. Make sure the presenters are not reading from their scripts.
6　Full rehearsal on the day at the venue.
7　Prepare a contingency plan in case something goes wrong with the demonstration.

This last point can be quite important. The product and equipment should be carefully checked before being put on public view. However, mistakes can occur. If something does go wrong, act immediately. You will not lose too much face if you deal with the situation efficiently and without embarrassment.

Shows and happenings

Occasionally something elaborate is called for; this could take the form of a fashion show, a song and dance routine or a playlet. However, tempting though these ideas may be, they should not be attempted without a professional producer and well trained performers.

There is nothing worse than an amateurish show or a badly produced spectacular. Sometimes industrially or trade oriented companies believe that a very gimmicky or sexy show will get them more coverage than a straightforward presentation or demonstration. This may be true of reaction within the sales organisation and the trade, but it is not true of journalists, particularly when there is likely to be a high proportion of women present.

The venue

Press conferences have been held in venues as diverse as Thames pleasure cruisers, converted warehouses and railway carriages. But of course hotels and restaurants are the more usual venues. Sometimes the conference is held at the company's own offices if they have premises in London. It goes without saying that except in special circumstances the reception will be held in London, as this is where the national media are based.

The right choice of venue is important to the success of any event. Here are some of the factors to consider in making your choice.

Budget limitations

London hotels and restaurants vary considerably in their banqueting prices and the first limitation on the choice of venue must be dictated by the available budget. It is of course possible to go to a relatively expensive venue and to keep the cost down by limiting the drinks to wine and keeping the food extremely simple.

On other occasions, however, you may want to offer a full bar service or a sit-down meal, and this can be achieved at a more reasonable venue which offers good food rather than expensive and luxurious surroundings. If the budget is really tight it may be worth considering a reception at breakfast or teatime.

Another way of saving money is to hold the reception in your own premises or in those of your advertising agent or PR consultant. Such premises can often offer facilities as good as those of a small hotel. The catering may be in-house or you can use an outside organisation to bring in an excellent buffet.

Suitability for the event

If you are planning a live demonstration or a show of some kind, you may need to look for a venue with special facilities such as a stage or a large demonstration kitchen. Some hotels have large ballrooms which can be used for this kind of event, but you will have to bring in everything else yourself and build a complete set.

The size and number of the rooms required will also have a bearing on your choice. You may, for example, want to keep the product to be presented under wraps until the last minute and this could mean receiving the guests in one room and then moving to another for the presentation and a third room for lunch.

If you have fixed upon a theme for the whole reception the venue should also fit the theme if possible. This might mean a health club, an art gallery or an outdoor venue – the latter, of course, with inside facilities for inclement weather! It could also mean taking over a wine bar or a restaurant which has an appropriate name and decor.

Proximity to Fleet Street

Journalists do not have unlimited time and they do not want to have to spend too much time travelling to and from a reception. 'Hard' news conferences should be held as near to Fleet Street as possible.Receptions may be held a little further away, but the West End is about as far as Fleet Street journalists will be prepared to go. Remember that when dealing with the consumer press 'Fleet Street' equally means 'Kings Reach', where the many IPC magazines are based.

Occasionally, successful receptions have been held further North or West and the transport problem has been solved by providing a bus from Kings Reach, but remember that heavy traffic can mess up the schedule. It is actually quite a good idea to provide transport for any reception which is held away from a direct bus or tube route from Waterloo or Fleet Street, but make sure that everyone knows that it is there and what time it will leave.

Curiosity value

Sometimes venues are chosen for their ability to attract a greater attendance, and there is no doubt that the first few receptions held at a new development like the Barbican, a new luxury hotel or a trendy restaurant do attract a good crowd. However, there is a limit to the effectiveness of this tactic. If the material to be imparted is of little interest the goodwill which has been generated by the choice of venue is soon dissipated. You should also be sure that the place is as good as it is reputed to be. A poor meal, slow service and rude waiters will have the same bad effect.

Some PROs have held press receptions on river boats and other unusual venues. This is all right if the venue does not move but if it does guest are trapped on board and cannot get off to go on to other appointments. If you plan this sort of trip make sure that your guests know that this will be the case.

Checklist for choosing a venue
Points to watch:

1 Cost of hiring the room and the cost of catering.

2 Type of food on offer and the ambience of the venue.

3 Location of the venue.

4 Size and suitability of the venue vis-à-vis the planned format for the reception.

Checklist: continued

> 5   Availability of the rooms for setting up and
>   rehearsal on the day, and possibly the day
>   before. How much will this cost?
>
> 6   Details of electrics, staging equipment and
>   other facilities.

Briefing staff

It is important that the hotel staff know exactly what is
going to happen and it is a good idea to have a
preliminary timetable typed out to give to the person in
charge of your reception. Any changes which may be
neccessitated by the late arrival of guests should then be
passed to the same person.

Signposting within the hotel is another point to watch.
Very often the only listing is in the main foyer and after
that the guests are left to find their own way down long,
tortuous corridors. It is easy to forget the name of the
correct suite and the invitation containing the information may have been left behind. A few signs are a
welcoming sight. But do make sure that the hotel
understands whose the reception is. If the event has
been organised by a PR consultancy they may use that
name rather than the client's name. This can cause
confusion when guests are thinking about attending a
reception for Brand X or Company Y.

The staff back at the PRO's office should also be
briefed on where the reception is being held, the
telephone number of the venue and how to get there.
One journalist recently recounted how she had rung up
the office of the PR consultant who had arranged a
reception to which she was invited to find out exactly
where the venue was. The reply was less than helpful;
first of all everyone associated with the account had gone
to the reception. There was no one in the office who
knew what the venue was, let alone where it was. The
receptionist/telephonist did not even have a phone
number to contact the staff if necessary!

The food and drink

The choice of food and drink will probably depend upon the size of your budget, but even if the budget is a large one an expensive multi-course meal with all the trimmings may not be the most appropriate choice. Certainly news reporters will not have the time to stay for very long after a conference, and a bar and sandwiches may be the most welcome choice.

It would also be quite wrong to assume that specialist editors and writers necessarily have more time on their hands. They will not thank you for keeping them for three hours or more on a product presentation followed by a long meal which does not start until 1.30 pm or later. A buffet will be much quicker and will enable those who have early afternoon appointments to have a snack and go on to their meetings.

A full-scale sit-down luncheon can be appreciated for high days and very special occasions, but make sure that everyone knows that this is the kind of event which could go on for some time. Otherwise the gaps at the table will start appearing even before the meal is served and will multiply as guests have to leave to meet their schedules.

Canapés and finger buffets

If you are serving alcohol you must serve some sort of food. This holds good whether you are offering a glass of champagne, a full bar, a cocktail or simply a glass of red or white wine.

Take care with the choice of food. It should be attractive and appetising but not too messy. Guests are unlikely to have plates for canapés and so most items should be bite-sized. Make sure there are enough paper napkins available and that there are plenty of waste baskets to discard them. Instruct the waiting staff to remove waste cocktail sticks, napkins, olive stones and so on from the tables frequently. Nothing looks worse than a littered canapé buffet.

Finger buffets will usually be served with plates, but many of the same considerations apply. Remember that guests will be juggling with plates, food, napkins and glasses all at once.

Fork buffets

This is probably the most popular form of catering for press receptions. There are a number of pitfalls which seem to catch out even the most experienced PROs quite regularly, so do check the following points very carefully.

Access to the buffet

Make sure that there are at least two, and preferably more, points of access to the buffet. Make sure, too, that guests realise they are there and use them. There is nothing worse than the huge queue which can form at a buffet for eighty or ninety guests.

Choice of food

The food must be easy to eat with a fork. Obvious, you probably think, but journalists get exceedingly annoyed by having to deal with unboned chicken dishes, chops and even huge chunks of beef which are too tough to cut with a fork.

Somewhere to sit

This is a 'must' if you are dealing with the women's press. There is nothing women journalists hate more than having to juggle with a plate of food, perhaps a roll and butter, a glass and a handbag in a very crowded room. Tables are a help but not obligatory. Chairs are essential.

Availability of different kinds of drink

Make sure that soft drinks and mineral waters are available for those who do not want to drink alcohol. If you have decided to limit the drinks to wine or beer and wine, do not have a bar in the vicinity and make sure that your own staff or that of your client company also keep within the restrictions. It is tactless for the MD to have a gin and tonic when everyone else is restricted to wine.

Sit-down meals

The main question here is whether to provide a formal seating plan or to allow guests to sit where they like. From the PRO's point of view, a seating plan could have the advantage of arranging for those journalists who are considered the most influential to sit close to the senior executives of the company. This is fine in principle, but very often it looks more like an exercise in impressing management with the calibre of the journalists attracted. It can also be rather invidious for those journalists who are not rated very highly and who will all find themselves on the lowest table in the room.

You will also be prone to glaringly obvious gaps left by absentees. However carefully your staff check on acceptances there will always be a crisis or two on the day and some people who had quite genuinely intended to come will not be able to. There will also be those who accept two invitations and finally choose the other.

A good compromise is to leave the guests to sit where they will but to reserve a seat on each table for a member of the host company and the PROs. Excess places can be cleared before the guests move into the dining room. Don't be too enthusiastic here; leave a couple of places for latecomers.

If you want to ensure that journalists with particular spheres of interest sit by the appropriate specialist, this can be arranged discreetly during the reception period and the people introduced before sitting down to lunch.

Breakfast, coffee and tea receptions

Although lunchtime is by far the most popular time for most kinds of press reception, there may be reasons why another time of the day would be more appropriate. For example, an early to mid-morning conference could be more useful for news reporters, and breakfast or teatime might be the time when the new product is mainly used. In general there should be a good reason for holding events at these times as they are not always so well attended.

Serving the client's product

Though it would seem to make sense to serve a new food product at its launch, this can be risky and it may be better to sample it before the luncheon or as part of the presentation. Very often products designed for domestic use do not lend themselves to catering in bulk and the hotel staff will not necessarily be used to dealing with them.

On other occasions the product to be launched is a sponsored book featuring a particular type of food or a range of products. Here there will probably be a number of dishes which, if carefully chosen, can be produced in quantity. But even here there may be problems, if the book features, for example, pasta; your guests will not want to eat pasta in every dish or at every course.

However, it is important to reflect the feel of the conference in the food. A very fatty lunch should not follow a seminar on the evils of high-cholestrol food, and product launch lunches for slimming foods or for health foods should use slimming ingredients or whole foods and not follow the example of a certain high fibre product launch luncheon which featured white bread, bland sauces, few vegetables and no fruit!

Guest list and invitations

The guest list should be drawn up in much the same way as you would draw up a mailing list for a particular press release (see Chapter 3). Only those who will have a genuine interest in the subject matter should be invited. Some PROs define this to mean only those who work for specific publications and consequently leave freelances off their guest lists. This can be short-sighted for two reasons. The first is that specialist freelances may be commissioned, at any time, to write a feature covering the area in which your product or service falls. If they do not have your information on file you may be left out. The second reason is that you never know where a freelance will appear next. Certainly a substantial number of female journalists take a few years off to have a family and will freelance in a desultory way during that time. Some may give up work or simply continue freelancing on an *ad hoc* basis, but others will attract major columns or will return to work as senior editors in their field. Ignore them and you may not suffer as a consequence, but help them and they will almost certainly help you when they are back at full strength.

Invitations

The invitation itself may be as simple or elaborate as the budget allows and you feel to be appropriate, though some journalists may be forgiven for thinking that the most elaborate invitations are actually a means of impressing the client or the boss rather than an attraction to the media.

In many cases a simple letter explaining what the conference is about will be sufficient. Of course urgent news conferences will be called by telephone. Some PROs design elaborate invitations which may reflect the theme of the conference but which do not give very much information. They then very often have to send a covering letter as well.

However, from the PR point of view there could well be a case for making an impact among the many invitations which hit the editor's desk. Unusual ideas have included a small orange tree plant for one of the citrus fruit information services, a recorded invitation on a small disc to a record launch and a printed handkerchief with a knot in it to a linen launch.

Include full details of the time and the venue with a map for anywhere which might be difficult to find. Give both the phone number and the address for replies and give as much information about the event as possible.

Reply cards and follow-up

Getting replies can sometimes be difficult and one way of encouraging journalists to reply is to include a reply card to fill in. Ideally this should be stamped; otherwise a phone call would be cheaper for the journalist or his publication. If you are saving money on the postage you may as well save some more by dispensing with the reply card.

Very often a phone-round by a junior member of staff will also be necessary to obtain a clear idea of numbers. But before complaining about the time and cost involved be sure that the invitations were really of value to the list you compiled. Too often the invitations received are of marginal interest to journalists and they will want to see how busy they are going to be on the day before deciding whether or not to attend your function.

Incidently, it's a good idea to check that the information given on the reply card is the same as that on the invitation itself and that the latter carries all the details required to get there. Sometimes they do not!

The press kit

As far as possible the press kit should contain all the details included in the presentation together with any relevant background material, photographs and samples. Below is an idea of some of the items which should be considered for inclusion. Try to separate the immediate story from the background information. (See Chapter 3 for detailed content of releases and captions and Chapter 5 for a discussion of the kind of samples to include and suitable giveaway material.)

Checklist for the press kit
1   Programme of events if the kit is to be handed
    out on arrival of the guests.

Checklist: continued

2	Press release on the salient points of the announcement, product launch or service.
3	Photographs.
4	The content of any speeches made by newsworthy speakers.
5	Background information on the market, product or company including recipes, hints and tips, etc.
6	Copies of any research used in the presentation.
7	Samples of the product.
8	Suitable giveaways.
9	List of stockists if appropriate.

Sometimes you may need to make up separate press kits for different sections of the media such as the trade press or the health press. These will include specialist material relevant to that particular group.

Where possible include everything in a single folder or binder and arrange for samples and kits to be packed into a suitable form of carrier. This will usually be a plain or printed carrier bag but could be a freezer bag, a hamper or a trolley, depending on the product under review.

Make sure that there are enough press kits. There is nothing more annoying to a journalist who takes the trouble to go to an event than to find that there is no material to take away. If you are not sure how many people will attend make up double quantity of kits. Those which are not taken up can be posted to any journalists who could not come.

Photographs, too, will need some extra thought. Not everyone will be able to use straight product shots, and shots with many accessories or those illustrating different uses of the product can come rather expensive in quantity. General shots may be too general for most publications and there will be no exclusivity. It is probably more sensible to think out all the most useful ways to picture the product and to display one copy of each photograph on a display board by the press desk. Journalists can be asked for their preferences as they leave and the photographs sent on. If there are a large number of pictures a printed request form may be useful.

Photographs displayed in this way are likely to be black and white. Colour shots can be discussed with individual journalists or a general offer to shoot special material made in the press kit.

Running the event

However brilliant the presentation and however good the food and wine, the smooth running of the event will depend upon detailed planning and careful organisation on the day. Here are some of the areas which can cause problems.

Venue arrangements

If you are launching a new product, arrange to keep it covered or in a separate room until the presentation, or you may lose some of your guests.

Check on the signposting arrangements, the provision of a press table and plenty of chairs, and the position of cloakrooms and toilet facilities. Make sure that all your staff can give directions to the latter. If the reception is in your own premises, make provision for coats, bags and umbrellas.

If there is to be a formal presentation make sure there is a gangway down the centre of the audience seats–it is possible guests may have to leave and the use of a central aisle causes less disruption than if they have to go all the way along a long row. Make sure, too, that members of the audience sitting at the back can see the speakers and any screens or displays over the heads of those at the front–a point often forgotten when the check is made in an empty room.

Arrange with the caterers to keep some food from the buffet for one or two latecomers and for celebrities, presenters and staff who may not be able to collect their food straight away.

Badges

To badge or not to badge guests can be a controversial question and there are those who will tell you that the press will not wear badges. Others are keen to badge everyone in sight. It is not true that the press will not wear badges.

The badges must be carefully prepared and their use limited to large gatherings where it is quite impossible to tell who is who. At small gatherings it can be useful to badge your own staff and that of your organisation or client but not the guests. Thus, everyone knows who will be able to answer questions. Make sure they can! For large gatherings differentiate between media and staff by giving different coloured badges.

If you are using badges choose the most convenient you can find and remember that women will be much more fussy about badges, as the material of their clothes is more easily damaged. Remember, too, that women tend not to have breast pockets. If you are using badges with pins make sure that the name is slotted in the correct way. If it is not it will be very difficult to do up the pin–a tiny point, but very annoying if you are the one trying to pin the thing the wrong way.

Badges are usually prepared in advance and handed out as guests arrive. To type them all on the spot usually means serious congestion at the door. However, journalists may arrive who have not replied or one person from a particular paper may turn up in a colleague's place. Hastily handwritten badges can make the journalist feel a little like a second class citizen–not a good idea if the substitute is a more senior member of the editorial team, which can often happen. A typewriter on the press desk will solve this particular problem.

It should of course go without saying that special care should be taken to check the spellings on badges.

Gatecrashers

If you are holding the reception or conference in one of the big London hotels you could have a problem with gatecrashers. There is a kind of grapevine about events and a journalistic fringe which tries to attend.

If you suspect a person of gatecrashing, approach the problem carefully and be polite. It is possible that you or your staff have missed the inception of a new journal. However, if you are reasonably certain that someone is trying to get in under false pretences, call the head waiter or manager supervising your event to deal with the problem for you. If necessary they will call the house detectives and make sure that the gatecrasher is removed. Indeed many of them are well known to the hotels.

Timing

This is an area about which most journalists complain. All too often an invitation says 12.00 for 12.30 and nothing happens until 1.15 or even later. This is completely wasted time for those who take the trouble to arrive punctually. The reason for the delay, of course, is that the PRO is waiting for journalists who are late. Very often the reason they are late is that they are tired of waiting for events to start–a circular situation and one which it is really up to the PRO to break. If you always start on time the problem will cure itself. Of course, to start with, you may have to put up with a steady trickle of latecomers, but word will soon spread and most people will start to arrive on time safe in the knowledge that they will not be kept waiting.

Make sure that all your own staff and those who are taking part in the presentation or demonstration also know the starting time. They need to be in place when you give the signal to commence.

Stand-by

The most useful stand-by you can have is a briefcase stuffed with all the things you might unexpectedly need. These include:

    pens and pencils
    paper clips
    Blu-tack
    sticky tape
    spare badges
    spare plug

and facts and figures on other aspects of your business which could come up at question time.

Follow-up

It's no good sitting back after a press conference and breathing a sigh of relief that it is all over. It isn't. The follow-up to the event is equally important in making sure that you get the most out of it.

All requests for information or pictures made at the event should be dealt with at once, before the journalist's enthusiasm has waned.

It is a good idea to carry a small notebook and pencil and jot down all the requests and ideas that come up in the course of your conversations at the event, and get your staff to do the same. Sound out ideas for feature material and special photographs and follow up any interest which has been expressed with a phone call the next day.

Indeed it is particularly important that you are in the office the next day, for this is when queries may come in which were not answered on the day. Interest is at its peak and you need to be there to encourage and help it along.

The signing-in book on the press desk will show the discrepancy between acceptances and attendances.

Press kits for those who were unable to attend should also go out at once, particularly to those people who asked for information to be sent. A kit arriving a week or so later does not show a great deal of enthusiasm on your part.

Summary of Chapter 9

1   Ask a number of searching questions to establish whether or not a press conference is necessary. Could the information be effectively communicated in any other way?

2   Decide upon the best timing for a press conference bearing in mind constraints such as the immediacy of the news story, the availability of products and personnel and the lead times for key media.

3   Decide whether the information to be imparted lends itself to a news conference, a photocall or a press reception and budget accordingly.

4   Define the main points to be communicated and choose a format which will best illustrate these points.

5   Plan the presentation or demonstration in detail and be as professional as possible.

6   Choose a venue to suit the occasion, theme or the content of the reception. Check the facilities with care and make sure that everyone is fully briefed.

7   Choose the most appropriate type of refreshment and make sure that it is easy to eat.

8   Invite only those journalists who will be genuinely interested in the material you have to offer.

9   Design invitations with impact but make sure that all the basic information together with full details of the event is also included.

10 Put together a press kit designed to be as informative

as possible. Consider the best way of offering photo-graphs.
11 Write a detailed checklist for the running of the event. Start on time.
12 Remember that helpful and efficient follow-up will yield even more coverage from the event.

Checklist for a press conference/reception

1 Once the date is final (see pages 135-7), check it with registers or journalists in your field.

2 Make up the guest list of journalists and/or photographers (see pages 158-9).

3 Work out the format for the event (see pages 139-42).

4 Book outside speakers, models, specialists as required.

5 Design, print and send out the invitations (see pages 159-60).

6 Work out the programme of events or time-table for the conference or reception (see pages 142-3).

7(a) Book the venue and give outline briefing to the banqueting manager, choosing menus and drinks etc.

(b) Book outside caterers.

(c) Brief in-house caterers.

8 Organise all products required for the demon-strations or for samples.

Checklist: continued

9(a)　Brief all the speakers and start to work on speeches or presentations.

(b)　Brief display designers for static displays.

(c)　Brief script writers and photographers etc. for audio-visual presentation.

10　Book photographer to cover the event.

11　If necessary, arrange for extra telephone lines, electric points etc.

12　Book amplification system and any other electrical equipment which will be needed.

13　Plan and make up the press kit (see pages 160-2).

The week before the event

14　Have signs and speakers' name plaques made up.

15　Organise and carry out rehearsals.

16　Brief telephone and reception staff at your company HQ or at the agency so that they know where the event is taking place and how to contact staff if necessary.

17　Follow up invitation to make up guest list.

18　Make up badges (see pages 163-4).

19　Double check everything to date.

On the day

20　Build displays.

21 Run through audio-visual presentations.

22 Final rehearsal of demonstration and live events.

23 Check the room arrangements in reception, presentation and eating areas.

24 Arrange speakers' name plaques on the speakers' table, check water and glasses.

25 Check all audio-visual equipment, microphones, lighting and electrics.

26 Check that all accessories, scissors, tape etc. are ready and in place for the event.

27 Brief the hotel staff on timing, drinks limitations etc.

28 Check the catering arrangements (see pages 155-8), availability of ash trays etc.

The day after

29 Send out press kits to all those who could not attend, with particular reference to those who asked for kits or who accepted and were unable to attend.

30 Follow up all noted requests for further information, photographs, mooted features and so on.

10 Seminars, workshops and teach-ins

Very often firms and organisations which are leaders in their fields possess information which could be of immense value to specialists in the media and, provided that it is not confidential in nature, there is a great deal of goodwill to be obtained by passing it on. The process of 'educating' the media, if carried out in the right way, can be a profitable experience at all levels. A seminar covering advanced technical processes aimed at senior editors and an ordinary teach-in on basic principles for young journalists possibly new to the field will both help to establish your organisation as *the* voice in the field.

Advanced seminars

At this level the seminar may have been conceived as a pooling of information within the industry, with representatives of different organisations such as universities, technical colleges and government departments present as well as researchers from the leading manufacturers. However, only the most informed of journalists is likely to benefit from an invitation to such a meeting, as the level of discussion is bound to demand the use of complicated scientific terms or technical jargon and the presentation may not be geared to explaining difficult points to those who are not so well versed in the subject.

However, the results and findings of such a meeting together with simplified summaries of any papers or reports could form the basis of an extremely useful advanced media seminar. Similarly the results of work within a single company, backed perhaps by a résumé of other work in the field, could provide an equally useful platform for an advanced seminar.

Subject matter and speakers

The most vital consideration is that you do have something of interest to say. It is even more important with this type of educative process than with general press conferences and receptions to avoid offering yet another elaborate puff for the company's products.

It is also important not to keep harping on the same old theme or you may find that new research or a change in trends in the market place have left you behind. You could look rather foolish. One organisation in the consumer field used to take every opportunity to criticise the health food lobby in their field. There were nutrition-based seminars and technical discussions 'proving their point'. However, when market trends shifted dramatically in the early 1980s others showed that their technical difficulties were not insurmountable and their nutritional arguments were at best biased and at worst incorrect.

Outside experts invited to speak at educational seminars alongside your own people, and even an informal discussion by specialists in opposing camps on controversial issues, will help to lend authenticity and authority to the event. You must make sure that the speakers know their subjects in depth. It is no good simply choosing people because they are attractive or well known, for they must be able to answer detailed questions from the more knowledgeable members of the media.

Advanced seminars are equally appropriate for educating all sections of the media and for use by all types of organisation. Industrially or technically oriented companies selling mainly to their own or other industries might cover technical or scientific advances, and in just the same way consumer-oriented organisations might cover advances in nutritional research or the current workings of computer technology. Here's a list of a few such seminars held over the last two or three years.

Light engineering

Advances in Machine Metallurgy: a seminar about the development of new materials which will help to prolong the life of certain factory machinery.

Safety at work

A seminar on the latest research into all aspects of safety on the shop floor.

Computer and micro chip manufacturing

Computers in the Home: The future
Revolution for the Eighties: The effects that microchip technology may have on domestic electrical appliances.

Food industry

Fibre: The current position, a look at the scientific background.
Chocolate flavoured chips: a look at modern flavourings technology.

Building industry

Built to last?: A look at trends in prefabrication techniques.

Health and beauty

Skin Deep: research into how the skin reacts to materials applied to it.

Insurance

Life Assurance, Endowments and Tax: the consumer story.
Protecting the Business: advanced insurance techniques for small business.

Most of these subjects are scientifically based or are based on the studies and opinions of experts within a particular industry. Sometimes market research can supply the material and in other instances such as fashion-based industries leaders of fashion or trend-setters will be the attraction. A very successful seminar was organised by a leading cosmetic company at the end of 1979. The subject was 'The 'Eighties Look'. Speakers were invited from France, Italy and the USA and the result was a most informative and lively seminar on fashion trends in these countries and in the UK. There was sufficient material for a number of the leading fashion and beauty editors to put together four or five quite different in-depth features.

Format

Despite the serious nature of advanced press seminars, do not underestimate the importance of entertainment value. The material may be brand new and very exciting, but if the speaker is unable to convey this to his audience the seminar has been wasted. Some experts are naturally good speakers, but others are not.

This kind of problem can be partially overcome by the use of good visual aids and demonstrations and here similar considerations apply to those covered on pages 147-50. Another way of helping to offset the bad speaker who is the only expert in his field is to spread the load. Invite two or three related experts and pick a chairman who is a good speaker and who can handle with tact both the panel of speakers and the audience. Incidentally the planning of visual aids or live demonstrations should act as a double check that you do have something of value to say.

Guest lists and invitations

Great care is needed in compiling a guest list for this kind of event. There is no point in asking journalists to give up a half or even a whole day unless it is truly going to be of value to them. There is no virtue in large numbers. A small audience of specialists will be much more valuable to all concerned. Their questions will be informed, and useful indications of areas in which more help is needed may come out of the discussion time.

A personal approach by telephone or with a long and detailed letter is the first step. You will need to explain exactly how much time will be involved, who the speaker or speakers are and the level at which the event is pitched. If you do not take the trouble to do this the invitation may be glanced at and passed on to a junior colleague who may not have the background to benefit from the seminar. Or the editor may come himself, mistakenly thinking that all will be over in a couple of hours or so. This happened at a high-powered engineering seminar, when the important guests had to leave for other engagements. They were as upset as the organisers but they had not appreciated the nature of the event.

A top-level seminar organised by a large industrial company could provide a valuable opportunity to invite foreign journalists or London-based representatives of foreign media. In the former case you will need to decide whether or not you will contribute towards travelling and accommodation costs. At the beauty seminar mentioned above, leading women's magazines in each of the countries represented were promised exclusive material if they attended, and the attendance costs were paid jointly by the magazines and the sponsor.

A useful book on the subject is *Planning & Organising*

Business Functions by Stuart Turner, published by Gower in 1983.

Checklist for an international advanced seminar
*Advance planning

1 Fix the date and book the speakers.

2 Book venue and organise catering arrangements.

3 Make any special arrangements with foreign media.

4 Make up guest list and send out the invitations.

5 Book simultaneous translation services and photographers.

6 Work out the programme for the seminar and put together the presentations, including speeches, visual aids and demonstrations.

7 Make travel and accommodation arrangements for speakers and media guests as required.

8 Make up general press kit for all media guests and exclusive material as appropriate.

*Planning just prior to the event

9 Check catering and accommodation arrangements.

10 Check the guest list.

11 Check arrangements and siting of translation booths, visual aid equipment, room layout, ash trays and water jugs, name plaques, air conditioning and lighting.

Checklist: continued

---

12 Prepare badges.

13 Rehearse all speakers and chairman or presenter.

14 Brief venue staff on timings.

15 Arrange positioning and manning of the reception desk.

*Planning for the day

16 Final rehearsals and checks.

17 Duplicate copies of speeches where possible for the translators.

18 Be on hand to stage-manage the seminar and to deal with problems as and when they arise.

*Have a look at the checklist for a press conference to jog your memory for items which you might have overlooked (see pages 167-9).

Workshops

Many of the points covered under advanced seminars are also relevant to workshops. These too are likely to take up more time than the average press conference and by their nature include involvement on the part of the audience. This may include cookery, make-up, decorating or other messy jobs and, though you will obviously be providing aprons, overalls, or other protective clothing, journalists will want to know in advance that they are expected to take part.

It is also important to let prospective guests know the level at which the workshop is pitched. Editors can then make sure that the right person is sent. Don't pretend a function is at a higher level than it is. If you do, you risk the editors never attending your functions again. Examples of successful workshops include:

Sponsor: Wallpaper and paint manufacturer
Subject: The use of a completely new type of wall covering
Guests: Do-It-Yourself specialists

Sponsor: Importers and suppliers of Chinese foods
Subject: Chinese cookery
Guests: Cookery editors and writers

Sponsor: Computer program specialists
Subject: Computerised accounts, forecast and stock control
Guests: Writers specialising in information for the small business.

Sponsor: Gardening tools manufacturer
Subject: Pruning methods
Guests: Gardening specialists

Teach-ins

On the whole teach-ins are aimed at the junior end of the media. Nowadays there is a good deal of moving about within a magazine group and a journalist could suddenly find him– or herself working on the technical page of a newspaper or the health and beauty department of a magazine while knowing little or nothing about the subject to be covered. There will of course be more senior people in the section, but they do not always have time to answer questions and will probably object to constantly being asked to explain things. Thus educational events organised by manufacturers and suppliers are usually welcomed by editors and appreciated by the juniors.

Subject and speakers

The subject matter at this end of the educational spectrum still needs to be interesting and fairly widely based, but it is likely to be much more unashamedly biased, with the sponsor's products being mentioned in some detail at the appropriate points. Do not, however, allow this aspect to take over from the general information, or no more juniors will be sent to you. The sort of subject headings which might be appropriate to the same areas as those given for advanced seminars are as follows.

Light engineering

Long-life Machinery: a teach-in on all the factors which affect the life of a machine, with a simplified version of the material on new metallurgical advances.
Safety at Work: a lower-level look at the factors which affect safety on the shop floor.

Computers and microchip industry

Using Computers in the Home; the current use of computers in the home with some information on possible future developments.
What Microchips Can Do: a look at their uses in domestic appliances and how they might be used in the future.

Food industry

Fibre in Food: what it is and what it does.
Flavour Faster: the current range of artificial flavourings and how they are produced.

Building industry

Prefabricated Housing: a look at the past and the future of this section of the industry.

Health and beauty

The Skin: the construction of the skin, how it works and how it reacts to skin creams, lotions and moisturisers.

Insurance

Life Assurance: what it is and how it works.
Insurance for Small Businesses: a basic look at the subject.

The speakers will probably be from within your own organisation and the atmosphere is usually much less formal than at an advanced seminar. The aim is to put young journalists at their ease so that they will enjoy the session and get the most benefit from it. However, care still needs to be taken with the format.

One manufacturer of products for use in hairdressing salons regularly holds seminars on hair structure and the effects of perming and colouring. The teach-ins are held in the company's own training school, where they have the latest equipment, and the manager of the school runs the session. She is a lively speaker and naturally knows her subject exhaustively. The only problem is that the young journalists get so interested and ask so many questions during the session that she finds it hard to get through the whole of the planned content! The session is backed up with live demonstrations on models and visual aids and includes a buffet lunch with wine.

If you are planning to run some teach-ins on a regular basis it is worth putting some care into their initial preparation. If possible carry out a dummy run to check timings and to look out for possible pitfalls. In some circumstances you may have to book a hotel room for the teach-ins, but if possible it is usually better to hold it on your own premises. The conference room or boardroom of the company may be pressed into service or the event could be held at the premises of your advertising or PR agency. The latter makes sense, as they will usually have visual equipment to hand.

The back-up material for this kind of teach-in can be very important for if it is presented in the right way the young journalist may continue to refer to it for some considerable time. If the subject is extensive it might be worth considering a loose-leaf file to hold the material. If this is set out in sections with general and technical information at the start of each section followed by details of relevant products, sections or pages which become out-of-date can be replaced by a simple mailing. This kind of in-depth reference can find a place on the journalist's permanent reference shelf.

Teach-ins can also be a source of ideas for feature material. Subjects which crop up regularly for questioning or discussion may be of equal interest to readers, listeners or viewers. Alternatively, you may be able to feed in your own feature ideas. Though the junior journalist may not be able to make the ultimate decision on a feature idea, he or she will be pleased to have ideas to offer their editors.

Checklist for a teach-in for young journalists

1   Agree date internally with speakers and organise venue.

2   Make up guest list and send out invitations.

3   Plan the content of the teach-in with the speaker or speakers and outside specialists, and book models if necessary.

4   Book caterers or alert internal catering staff.

5   Make up visual aids and rehearse the presentation if it has not been given before.

6   Make up press kit for journalists to take away.

Seminars for one

This may sound rather a contradiction in terms, but it is a technique used by one multinational organisation in all its dealings with the corporate and financial media and is well worth considering if your organisation is in a similar position.

The whole of the media relations programme is concerned with corporate and financial issues and everything is carried out on a one-to-one basis. There are no receptions and no press releases. The news wire services are used for the transmission of information, since the post is too slow.

The target audience is relatively small, being confined to specialist writers and editors on the national dailies and foreign dailies, a specialist magazine or two and senior TV and radio producers in each of the main countries within which the company operates.

The needs of each individual section of the target audience are carefully analysed and a package is put together for each one. This may involve a visit to a foreign depot, an in-depth interview with the US managing director, a fact-finding tour of the South American operation or the setting up of a discussion group within the computer development group. There is no speculative entertaining. If a journalist is invited to lunch the PRO always has a special feature or idea in mind. Such activities take some time to arrange and the programme is long-term. It is impossible to be ambitious on this kind of time schedule and the company takes a long view.

Even when there is a more immediate message, such as the company results, to be communicated, the contact is still one-to-one. Six or seven key journalists are selected; they are offered an appointment with the managing director on the day the results are announced. Each journalist is thus able to ask his own questions and build up his own angle without having his ideas heard by other journalists and perhaps used in a rival publication. The rest of the media get the bare bones of the information on the news wire.

The selected journalists are telephoned in advance to see if they would like to take up the offer of specific exclusive comments and an appointment is made. The order in which the representatives of the leading publications see the MD is varied each year. The result of this careful planning is a much larger number of in-depth comments on the results than is normally the case.

Summary of Chapter 10

1   The process of 'educating' the media, both at the senior and at the junior level, can be highly valuable to both your organisation and the media.

2   Your firm or organisation may possess information which could be of great value to specialist journalists. Provided that it is not confidential this research or expertise could form the basis of an advanced seminar for senior journalists and specialist writers.

3   Remember that the subject matter of such seminars must have real depth and should be presented by the experts themselves.

4   Advanced seminars can be used to equal effect by industrially based companies and by consumer-oriented organisations. Successful subject headings are listed.

5   Plan the format of an advanced seminar with interest and entertainment value as the main criteria. It may be necessary to consider audio-visual aids or live demonstrations.

6   Limit guest lists to those with a genuine interest in the subject and set out the nature and length of the event on the invitation.

7   Planning is vital to the success of such events, so check the sample checklist.

8   Workshops where journalists are encouraged to take part are a natural extension of the advanced seminar.

9   Teach-ins for junior journalists can be equally useful

in educating newcomers to a particular field both in the general principles of the subject and in the contribution made by your own organisation.

10 Plan content in detail; similar considerations will apply here to those for advanced seminars. Ideas for a simplified or lower-level presentation are given for the same markets as those listed for advanced seminars.

11 Think about the use of follow-up material as a permanent reference.

11 Special events

From time to time it may be useful to invite journalists to your own premises or to exhibitions or sporting events. The reasons for such visits could be many and varied. You may want to show off a new and quite different system of warehouse control, the company may be opening ultra-modern showrooms or premises in a brand new city centre shopping precinct, you may be presenting a new product at a trade exhibition, or you may simply want to show specialist writers exactly what your operation involves.

Sponsored sporting events, new machinery installations, historical exhibitions and unusual laboratory techniques might also form the basis of a special event or a press visit. But what ever it is, the visit must be well thought out, carefully planned and efficiently executed. The arrangements for the whole trip will be part of the PR showcase for your organisation or company.

Initiating the visit or event

As usual, the first question to ask is whether or not there is a valid reason for inviting the media. Is there a newsworthy story? Will a visit provide really useful in-depth background material? Are there misunderstandings or misconceptions which such a visit could clear up?

Sometimes there are other, internal, reasons for staging a special event–but it can also be used to get to know specialist writers rather better. For example, a factory opening will be important to local community relations, but the London-based trade press may also be interested. Or a sponsored sporting event which is part of the marketing department's promotional strategy, could also be useful for entertaining influential specialists who might enjoy a day out. In each case there will also be other journalists who will be specifically interested, such as the local media representative in the case of the factory opening and the sporting press in the case of a sponsored event. These must not be forgotten.

The next step, therefore, is to decide who might be interested in a visit or in attending a special event. If the answer coincided with the list of people you would particularly like to know better, then you are in business. Following the opening of Tadchester New Town Development Zone, for example, the PR consultant decided to institute a series of visits to the town to see the progress made and to talk over some of the controversial points which had arisen out of the government's new policy. Invitations were issued to the industrial editors of the national dailies and over a period of six months five leading journalists in the field visited the area.

In quite different circumstances, a light engineering company wanted to improve its standing in the community, which had suffered a bad blow following an industrial accident. The premises were thrown open for a public open day and staff were encouraged to show their families round the works. The event was used not only to show the local media the processes which were carried out in the factory and the high level of safety precautions, but also to invite specialist writers from the industry's trade press and the technical pages of the *Financial Times* and the *Daily Telegraph,* all of whom attended.

Planning

Detailed planning is essential for the success of any kind of visit or event. So the first job after ensuring that your potential guests are able to come is to work out a programme of events and to brief everyone concerned. Here are some points to watch which apply to most types of events, however large or small.

Travel arrangements

To some extent these will depend upon how far away you are from London or from the local and regional media. It will also depend upon the journalists' own inclinations. Some people prefer to drive themselves to this kind of event. Others do not want to drive at all.

The choice of transport includes coaches, trains and aircraft. The latter will, of course, have to be used if your premises are a long distance from London. If you are near to an airport scheduled flights can be used, but there may be occasions when you will need to consider hiring a private plane. Helicopters can also be hired at surprisingly reasonable costs if speed is essential over shorter distances.

For medium distances trains will probably be the answer, perhaps backed up by a coach or cars to meet guests at the station and drive them to your premises. Tickets and seats can be booked in advance and sent to guests. Make sure that you have someone on the train to welcome them and to look after refreshments on the journey.

The question of refreshments can cause some problems, for unless you make special arrangements and book a whole coach it is not possible to book in the restaurant car, and if all your guests want to have breakfast or dinner on the train it will not be easy to seat them altogether.

The PRO of a cosmetic company solved this problem on a journey to Lancashire for a factory opening by making up strong cake boxes containing continental breakfasts with orange juice, fresh croissants, butter and jam, and organising coffee from the buffet. A more elaborate breakfast or dinner might have been obtained from one of the many small catering companies which have sprung up in recent years.

For short and medium journeys a mini-bus or coach can make the journey much easier. This is particularly useful if your premises are rather inaccessible or necessitate a change or two on public transport. Modern coaches are very comfortable and some even have bars and toilet facilities on board.

Remember that it is equally important to have a member of your staff on board to brief the driver, welcome and check off the guests and if necessary decide whether or not to leave without a latecomer.

Tour itineries and guides

If your guests are to tour the factory or premises do not just leave things to chance or to a spur-of-the-moment initiative. This certainly will not work if the group is too large to go round in one batch, and it could lead to trouble even if you are the guide.

Work out the route in advance, taking into account the likely timings on important processes, tea and coffee breaks and the production schedule for the day. You should organise the tour so that the visitors have the most interesting time possible. It usually makes sense to start at the beginning of the production process, following the items through to completion, but it is worth breaking out of the logical progression if there is something which can only be seen at a particular time of the day.

Check the specialist interests of your guests and then go and talk to the factory managers, briefing them as fully as possible and taking their advice. They will know their own production lines far better than you will. This means that their advice should also be taken on guides for the party.

One guide should not be asked to take more than six or seven people, and if the factory is a noisy one the number should be even smaller. There is nothing more irritating to a journalist on a visit than not being able to hear what is being said when faced with an array of unfamiliar machines.

Once the tour itinerary has been agreed, write it down and time it. The written itinerary can then be passed to anyone who might have to take over the tour at the last minute and the time will also help you to plan the rest of the day. You may want to organise a discussion group or arrange for individual journalists to meet specialist members of staff. Then of course there is lunch to fit in and public transport timetables to bear in mind.

If you have a large party of journalists it is a good idea to brief the guides on what to expect. A party made up of consumer journalists, for example, will put quite different questions to those which can be expected from trade or industrial journalists, who will be much better informed about the techniques and processes involved. Make sure that all the guides appreciate the good points which can be conveyed about your operation, such as an increasing labour force, re-cycling of waste materials, quality control procedures and environmental awareness.

Catering arrangements

At special events and exhibitions you will probably be limited to the caterer who has the concession for the venue. However, thought still needs to be given to the choice of food and drink to be served. The same kind of considerations will apply as those discussed on pages 155-8 for press conferences and receptions.

If the event is on your own premises you will need to choose between your own catering staff, if any, outside caterers and local hotels and restaurants. Your own canteen staff may be annoyed if you resort to outside people. On the other hand they may not be able to cope with the extra load. The sensible thing is to approach them first and get them to participate in the decision.

In some areas the choice of outside caterers may be limited, while in others there may be plenty. Whatever the situation, check them carefully and if you have reservations at all keep the catering simple.

Local hotels and restaurants are generally only used if there are a few guests. Some companies, of course, have a standing rule that all guests are entertained in the staff canteen. This is fine if the food is of a high standard, but a journalist will not be happy to travel maybe a hundred miles or more for a sub-standard canteen lunch, particularly if you are the one who wants to disperse misapprehensions or get to know a specialist writer.

Local hotels will, of course, have to be used if you are so far from London that the journalist will need to stay overnight. Here again it pays to find out which is the most pleasant to stay in.

Visits

Here are a typical programme and checklist for a factory visit for a small group of journalists coming both from London and from the local media.

Programme

	am
Coach arrives at pick-up point in Central London	9.00
Pick-up for guests	9.00–9.30
Journey to factory premises; coffee served from flasks en route	9.30–11.15

Arrive at factory premises and welcomed by the general manager, shed coats and don overalls	11.15–11.20
Tour round the factory	11.25–12.30 pm
Buffet luncheon and wine in the boardroom, joined by the directors	12.30–1.30
Presentation on developments to come followed by question time	1.30–2.15
Tour of the development laboratories	2.15–2.45
Visit to the factory shop	2.45–3.00
Tea served in the boardroom	3.00–3.30
Coach takes guests back to London	3.30–5.45

The programme is flexible enough to allow extra time at various points of interest if required. Tea– or lunchtime will simply be shorter.

Checklist for a visit

1   Send out invitations and check responses.

2   Brief factory manager and discuss itinerary and guides.

3   Book coach and send out details of travel arrangements and pick-up point. Send time-table and maps if necessary to local journalists.

4   Brief development manager and arrange tour of laboratories.

5   Write script for development presentation and sort out slides or flip charts to go with it.

Checklist: continued

6   Organise catering with canteen staff and if necessary outside caterers.

7   Brief managing director and board members on arrangements over lunch, provide guest list and book the boardroom.

8   Arrange for a member of staff to be on the coach and work out how to organise coffee on the coach.

9   Inform reception that two journalists will be arriving separately from the main body and arrange car parking.

10 Make sure that there is a large enough selection of white overalls to fit various sizes and that there are safe cloakroom facilities for guests' coats.

11 Alert all staff to the visit via the factory and office notice boards.

12 Check the catering arrangements on the day clean glasses, paper napkins, soft drinks etc.

13 Rehearse the presentation with the presenter and check visual aids.

14 Agree any special prices or discounts with the factory shop manager.

15 Put together press kit of background material, booklet samples etc. and place on the coach on arrival for distribution during the return journey.

16 Check radio broadcasts in the morning for
traffic delays, weather changes etc. which
might affect the visit.

17 Make sure you are there the moment the coach
arrives, stay with the guests until they leave
and be ready to sort out any small snags which
may arise during the day.

Openings

The first consideration here is who to perform the
opening ceremony. You may decide that the opening is
not of any great significance beyond your local area. In
this case the managing director or the chairman may
want to do the honours. On the other hand, you may
want to emphasise the company's local ties, in which
case the mayor or a leading councillor may be invited to
perform the ceremony. Local celebrities offer further
choice.

If, on the other hand, the opening represents a great
step forward in new technology, a big rise in export
orders or a very timely increase in employment in the
area, the story might have national appeal. If so the
company may decide to invite a national figure to open
the premises.

If it looks as though this might happen, planning
should start in very good time indeed. Celebrities tend to
be booked up quite a long way in advance; this is
particularly true of 'Royals' or senior members of the
government. In the latter case remember that cabinets
can be reshuffled, so make sure that the invitation is to
the minister rather than the individual, unless there is
some personal connection which would mean that the
person should be present in any case.

The royal family nearly always provide news value, and
government ministers may take the opportunity to make

a statement of importance and so are quite likely to attract the media. Of course a significant statement could detract from your own event, but that is a risk you have to take and, provided that you have briefed the minister's staff well, any such statement could be very relevant to your own news.

If you are a sportswear manufacturer a leading sportsman in the field might be another idea, or if you manufacture video or TV equipment you might go for a TV personality. However, care should be exercised in this area. An unrelated star can sometimes be interpreted by the media as the sign of a weak story.

Almost as important as the choice of celebrity is the back-up plan in case the chosen celebrity is unable to turn up on the day. Government ministers are particularly prone to this kind of cancellation, for they never know what issues are suddenly going to arise which need their immediate attention.

A company organising the opening of a big new factory development in the North East was faced with just this problem. A phone call came from the minister's private secretary at 6 o'clock on the evening before the ceremony was to be performed. The PRO immediately contacted the local MP, who had helped to arrange the minister's visit. Unfortunately he too had to remain in Westminster for an emergency debate. In the event the mayor of the local town agreed to perform the ceremony. He had already accepted an invitation to attend and was happy to step into the breach.

The opening ceremony itself also needs to be planned in some detail. Where will it take place? Is there room for everyone to see the ceremony and what will happen if it rains?

Openings will also normally include a factory tour and some form of refreshments, and the plans outlined on pages 187-9 should be equally useful here.

Here are a typical programme and checklist for a full-scale factory opening.

Programme

	am
Meet London-based journalists at Kings Cross	7.30–8.00
Train leaves London	8.00
Train arrives local town with coach pick-up	10.20
Coach arrives at premises	10.55
VIP guests welcomed and coffee served	10.45–11.15
Opening ceremony performed with short speeches	11.15–11.30
Tour of site/premises/factory	11.30–12.15
	pm
Pre-lunch drinks	12.15–12.30
Luncheon served	12.30–2.00
Coach leaves for station	2.00–2.35
Train leaves for London	2.45
Train arrives London	5.10

Checklist

1 Guest to perform opening ceremony decided upon and invited with fallback worked out.

2 Order commemoration plaque if required.

3 Site for opening ceremony agreed.

4 Guest list drawn up and invitations produced and dispatched.

5 Design and produce any display material needed.

6 Marquee booked if required.

Checklist: continued

7 Catering arrangements agreed and booked (see pages 188-9).

8 Public address system booked.

9 Travel arrangements put in hand, coaches booked, drivers briefed and the journey timed (see pages 186-7).

10 Guided tour arrangements put in hand (see pages 187-8).

11 Photographer booked, possibly including videotape.

12 Alert staff to the preparations and arrange for as many as possible to witness the ceremony.

13 Supervision of erection of the marquee, installation of electrics etc.

On the day

14 Make up press kit and remember to add copy of main speaker's speech.

15 Set aside a room for the press to telephone stories to their offices and another room for radio or press interviews.

16 Check catering arrangements.

17 Rehearse ceremony.

18 Have to hand all items required for opening ceremony curtains: ribbons and scissors, spade and tree etc.

Checklist: continued

---

19 Cordon off area where the ceremony is to be performed and leave space for photographers, organise lighting if necessary.

20 Prepare badges for staff attending the ceremony.

21 Organise reception area, cloakroom etc. for guests and press.

22 Organise table seating plan if formal meal.

23 Generally stage-manage the day, making sure all members of staff involved are in the right place at the right time.

Exhibitions and shows

Setting up and organising an exhibition or show stand is beyond the scope of this book, but exhibitions are often used to launch and demonstrate new products and can therefore offer an opportunity of showing the relevant sections of the media new developments in action without them having to go to distant factories. The experts will also be on hand to talk about the product. This sort of activity works just as well for heavy farm equipment or light engineering equipment as it does for consumer products or systems for small businesses.

Here are some points to watch when holding a press reception or even inviting individual members of the press to an exhibition stand.

Make sure that your guests will be able to get in easily. You should not assume that they will all have press tickets or that their press card will give them automatic entry. If you speak to the organisers they should let you have the requisite number of press passes or they may send them out for you.

Nor should you assume that it is sufficient simply to give the number of your stand. Places like Earls Court, the Birmingham Exhibition Centre and the Royal Show are very large and it can be a nightmare wandering round trying to find the right stand. So send a catalogue or a map with the tickets.

Some important exhibitions are held outside London and if you are planning a press reception at one of these you should consider offering to pay the train fare for those journalists you really want to attend. Indeed, if you are not prepared to do this you should not invite anyone. Not all magazines will pay for their staff to cover out-of-town exhibitions and freelancers have to pay their own way. The offer of free travel will help to ensure a good attendance.

Some companies object to paying fares on the grounds that other manufacturers at the exhibition may benefit, since the journalist is likely to take the opportunity to look round the exhibition while he or she is there. This is a rather shortsighted view, for journalists do remember those PROs who help them. They may give coverage not on that particular product at that time, but on a future item or when information or pictures are needed for a particular story or feature.

It may sound rather obvious to say that you should ensure that the stand is finished in time for the press day or press preview but it is surprising how many are not–even though the press have been invited to an exhibition breakfast or luncheon. Demonstrations and displays must be finished and in working order or the visit will be a waste of time for the journalist.

It's also quite a good idea to check on what other stand holders are doing. Talk to the exhibition press officers, who usually know what has been planned, and either get in first or arrange your reception around the others. Make sure, too, that all your material is prominently displayed in the press room.

Sponsored events

Very often invitations to sponsored events are actually a way of saying 'thank you' for support during the year, though in some instances there is a definite link between the sponsored event and the sponsor's product. Sponsored events can also have a high degree of news value in their own right. A paper manufacturer, for example, sponsored a nationwide children's painting competition; the display of the finalists' work attracted considerable media attendance.

Most of the same considerations apply to sponsored events as to visits, openings and exhibitions. In addition it is essential to make sure that guests have tickets. Race courses and sporting arenas, for example, will not allow journalists in on the flash of a press card, so the press will need to have the correct tickets for the various enclosures. It is probably worth a confirmatory phone call a day or two after you have sent off tickets, maps etc. If the worst comes to the worst you will then be able to arrange for your guests' names to be left at the gate with an authorisation for entry.

Summary of Chapter 11

1   It can be useful to invite journalists to visit your own premises or to attend exhibitions or sponsored events organised by the company.
2   Is there a valid reason for such a visit, and if so who would be most interested in taking part?
3   Detailed planning is essential to the success of such ventures and should take into account the following areas: travel, tour itineraries and guides, and catering arrangements.
4   The choice of some one to perform opening ceremonies can be critical and a number of factors must be taken into account.
5   Exhibitions or shows can provide useful opportunities for demonstrating new products. Points to watch include

provision of entry tickets, travel arrangements and liaison with the exhibition's own press office.
6   Sponsored events such as race meetings and other sporting events, cultural activities and exhibitions may also involve entertaining the media. Many of the same factors apply here as for visits, openings and exhibitions.

12 Educating management

Public relations executives do not work in a vacuum, and the activities of the PR department are very much a part of the marketing strategy of the company. However, it is important to remember that these activities may also be concerned with the shareholders' view of the company, with local and employee relations in and around the company's premises, and with other issues regarded as important by the board or the managing director, such as the environmental image of the company, the perceived place of the company within its own industry, and, perhaps, the need to further certain government legislation.

The marketing department

The marketing department staff, with the possible exception of the marketing director, are working in a much narrower field and tend to believe that the PR function is solely there to back their efforts in the market place. This can sometimes lead to misunderstandings and clashes, for the PRO must watch over all aspects of the company's image and objectives.

What constitutes news value

The concentration of the brand or marketing manager on his own range of products can make it difficult for you to point out that the publicity potential of a particular brand does not necessarily equate with that brand's importance to the company. Sixty per cent of the company's business may be in an everyday line which has not changed for years. The other 40 per cent is made up of two or three other reasonably strong lines, with 10 per cent specialist products and new products on trial.

The marketing manager is quite naturally keen to keep up the interest and coverage on the line with 60 per cent of the sales. He is quite convinced that a minor change to the product or new packaging is rivetting news and he probably wants a big press conference on the subject. He does not much like the idea of concentrating on one of the new or specialist products which, he believes, does not generate the income to pay for much press activity.

As an experienced PRO you know that a conference on such meagre grounds will not be successful and as tactfully as possible you must point out that the media have to take a much wider view and that there is very little news value in the changes which have been made. On the other hand the new or specialist product, or maybe a selection of them, do have a good deal of intrinsic interest and an event geared to them will project the company image as innovative and go-ahead. It will also promote the company or brand name and the bread-and-butter lines will benefit from the publicity for the other more newsworthy areas.

An alternative suggestion is to look for material which could be used for an educational event, such as a seminar or a teach-in. In this instance the everyday line could be brought in at the appropriate point along with other relevant products. The exercise is again one of image-building and all the company's products will benefit from it.

This kind of problem can be even more difficult to solve if there are two or three brand or marketing managers, each with their own range of products and their own budgets. Inevitably they will be competing with each other and will be even more reluctant to see PR activity directed towards their rival's products, with rather less coming their way.

Part of the solution lies in making sure that these managers understand what the media are looking for. To some extent this varies depending on the section of the media concerned. However, in specialist and trade areas it is quite easy to show that hard facts and significant changes or advances are at the top of the list. A brand new type of material for joining sections of piping, a breakthrough in plastics technology or the opening of a new plant to manufacture bio-chemicals for the medical world make hard news in this area of the media.

Indeed a glance at the trade and technical magazines covering an industry plus the specialist pages in the national press will show the sort of material required. So make sure that your brand managers receive these publications, point out significant material to them and suggest that they listen to relevant radio and TV programmes. Once they understand what is required they will be in a much better position to supply you with the right sort of material to attract media attention. Discussions will be based less on comments like 'Why haven't we had as much coverage as X?' and more on 'How about building a feature round the new quality control techniques which have been instituted?'

The consumer press is usually far more of a mystery to management. Managers tend to see gimmicks as a bait here and also often equate their sometimes very much smaller organisations with the big multinationals, which do appear in the consumer press quite often. The need here is to explain the size and scope of the material being dealt with at national level. Everything needs to be a little more interesting or newsworthy in order to attract attention. The idea that accompanying a boring release with a bunch of flowers will ensure its immediate translation into print must be squashed.

False expectations

False expectations are one of the commonest problems with which a PRO has to deal. People working very closely with a range of products or services will quite naturally tend to think that those products are very important and will be angry if they are left out of a review article–which, indeed, could be your fault!

Nevertheless false expectations are a perennial bugbear. They take a variety of forms including:

- Expecting a massive attendance at a press event.
- Expecting everyone who comes to use the material.
- Expecting guaranteed coverage of everything in the press release, particularly if it is a fairly good story.
- Expecting immediate impact.

Quite apart from an excessive belief in the product, these expectations are unrealistic because they do not take account of how the media work. Here are a few points which should be made against each of the expectations listed above.

Size of attendance

Attendance will depend upon the strength of the story and what else is happening on that day. You must make management understand what makes a good story. It is then your task to convey the fact that there is something worth listening to and check the dates to minimise the chances of a clash with publication dates or other events.

Very often management complain if the editor does not come in person but sends a junior. There could be a variety of reasons for this–he or she may just have a previous engagement. It does not necessarily mean you will not receive good coverage, which the junior could be just as capable of providing.

Use of material

If the story is good the chances are that most people, if the guest list was correctly chosen, will use material. However, coverage depends not only on the story and the way it is presented but also on what else is happening at the time, on the subject matter of features which have already been planned months ahead and on space variations in the publications.

It is also important to point out that the journalist or photographer who attends your event may not have the final decision on whether or not the piece is used. It is fairly common to find, on borrowing a print which has not been used from a newspaper picture desk for use in your own house journal, that it has been marked up for publication. It had obviously been 'spiked' at the last minute.

Amount of material used

Most journalists who are doing their job properly will re-write material given to them and it is up to them to assess the relative importance of the material in the light of the space they have. Obviously mistakes should be corrected, but it is unrealistic to expect your every word to be included.

The use of, or rather the omission of, brand names also causes problems. Some publications *never* use brand names and you will simply have to point out to management that this is a policy decision which you can do nothing to change. What you can do, however, is to present the material in such a way that it is obviously your brand which is being referred to. If your product is so much like everyone else's that it cannot be identified in this way it probably has little news value anyway.

Timing of coverage

Here again management needs to understand that publications have quite different lead times. Some may be only a few hours or a day, whereas others will be two or three weeks or as much as three to six months. This inevitably means that the coverage gained will not come all at once.

Reluctance to release information

An understanding of this last point, the differing lead times of the media can help the PRO tremendously when it comes to releasing material in advance of a big launch. Advance release may be out of step with the marketing timetable but the strategic planning of a press campaign will certainly come to nothing if it is not understood.

Even if you cannot get agreement for the advance release of information to the consumer media, it is essential that you obtain permission to talk to the trade press about the developments. All too often the marketing department digs its heels in and refuses to release any information to the media until the marketing and sales campaign is launched. However, they are prepared to brief the sales force and, once they have been told, half the industry knows. The trade press may then find themselves in the very embarrassing position of bringing out a story after everyone has heard it. They may also learn of it from people other than those in your own organisation and may release an inaccurate version of the story. They will blame you in either situation.

The fear of information leaking from the trade media is generally unfounded. Journalists in this area will respect your confidence, for if they do not they know they will not be trusted again. The fear of a leak is usually unreal; if the information is so important to competitors they can probably learn it by other means than pumping the trade press.

Secretiveness can also lead to other problems with

various sections of management. No journalist is going to publish possibly exaggerated claims about the position your company holds in the market, about the public's view of your products, or about export trade figures unless he can see hard statistical information to back up such claims.

Some marketing managers are loath to hand over valuable market research information to competitors via the trade press. They feel that, having spent money which others have not, they should keep the information to themselves. There is something to be said for this view. On the other hand the publication of at least some of the findings could substantiate claims which might otherwise be disregarded, and could also help to enhance the reputation and stature of the company within the industry.

The less obvious aspects of good media relations

It can be even more difficult to make management understand that some of the PR budget should be spent on educational events or even on entertainment which will not yield an immediate result. A good deal of PR activity is long-term in its effect. You may want to build up relationships with key media or to educate specialists about the more esoteric parts of the business. Sometimes rather than achieving a glowing report the success will lie in preventing adverse publicity.

Other departments

Of course there are many marketing people who do understand the workings of the media, but there may be other people within the company who will come into contact with the media in the course of receptions, visits and exhibitions and it will be equally important that they too have an understanding of what you are doing and what you are trying to achieve.

Many people have preconceived ideas about journalists themselves. There are those who subscribe to the view that journalists are all incipient alcoholics who mostly have nothing better to do than talk to contacts over a beer or a gin and tonic. Others view the women's interest press as jolly little girls playing at being journalists and others still who believe that anyone in the media is intent on attacking them.

The result of these ideas can be an extremely unfortunate attitude which shows itself either in fear of speaking to the media at all or in a patronising way of speaking which would alienate anybody. So do make sure that the MD does not keep harping on the idea that everyone just cannot wait to get to the bar, that the production director does not gloss over the technical detail of how grummits are made, and that the sales director does not talk down to the cookery journalist who he believes may understand the home but not the market.

Such briefings must also include the points set out on page 202. However, the most important point to convey to everyone who is speaking to the media is that they should tell the truth. There is absolutely no point in lying or in trying to cover up a possibly unpalatable truth. It will catch up with you in the end. As PRO you should be advising your management on the best possible presentation of the truth so that facts are given in the right context to enable the public to understand what your company is doing and why.

You must make management understand that if you do not put all the facts forward someone will ask the relevant question, for journalists are informed about their field, and then they will wonder why you did not volunteer the information in the first place. Sometimes the reasoning behind such withholding of information is simply misguided rather than deceitful. At a conference to announce a new standard in the presentation of a raw food the presenters decided that the detail of how the standard was achieved might be something of a 'put-off' and glossed over that part of the process. Inevitably the question was asked and the answer given. The facts were actually quite acceptable and the effect was that the journalists were left with a nagging doubt as to whether or not they had been told the whole story. They had, but it would have been far better to include everything at the outset.

How to educate staff and management

A number of useful ploys will help to make your internal educational programme easier. At the more junior levels an invitation to accompany you on activities such as a photographic session for feature material, a local radio broadcast, an individual journalist's visit to the factory or even a trip round a newspaper or magazine office and printing press can all help to show how the media work and what journalists' requirements are. If the executive knows nothing at all about PR, a briefing session beforehand will be useful, and you might also warn any journalists concerned what you are doing.

This job can be a little more difficult with senior executives. However, you may be able to ask a good friend or two from the media to join you both for lunch. This will enable you to talk informally about the requirements of the media and the manager will be getting the facts 'straight from the horse's mouth'. Once it is seen that you do know what you are talking about, it will be much easier to make senior management listen to you in future. It will also be easier for you to make sure that management makes a more realistic assessment of the work you do and the coverage you achieve.

Assessing PR

All too often public relations is judged on the same sort of criteria which would be used to judge an advertising campaign. Unfortunately it is difficult to relate PR activity to sales leads, let alone sales. There can be some feedback from the trade press, particularly if a magazine runs a reader information service, but these are by no means universal.

Column inches are the obsession of some managers and the press relations service is often judged on the volume of these. Some managements demand monthly totals translated into advertising costs. But this is not a particularly good way of assessing results. Your own continuous assessment is much more important, not just at the beginning or at the end of the year but throughout the programme. Ask yourself why you are doing what you are doing. What are your objectives? Who are you trying to reach and what are you trying to tell them? Are you using the right tools and the right media to achieve these objectives? Is it working and what can you learn from your success or failure so far?

This kind of assessment will make it much easier for you to maintain your position. Remember you are the expert and you must insist on what you believe is the professional thing to do.

Checklist: do's and don'ts for management education

Do's

1 Remember that the media relations programme does not operate in a vacuum. You will need the co-operation and understanding of all departments.

2 Try to show management good news stories in the relevant media and discuss how such stories can be found in your own organisation and its activities.

3 Arrange informal meetings between management and friendly journalists so that each group can talk about their problems.

4 Make sure that management knows what can be realistically expected from press functions and visits.

Checklist: continued

5   Work at removing preconceived ideas about journalists and their behaviour.

Don'ts

1   Expect management to understand about lead times, press dates and space problems if you make no effort to inform them.

2   Arrange media conferences, meetings or visits without first fully briefing all those members of staff who will come into contact with the guests.

3   Allow your management to lie to the media.

Index